APRIL 25 THROUGH MAY 26, 2001

ROBERT MILLER GALLERY

524 WEST 26 STREET NEW YORK 10001

TEL.212.366.4774 FAX.212.366.4454

WWW.ROBERTMILLERGALLERY.COM

JOAN SNYDER

PRIMARY FIELDS

PRIMARY FIELDS

The beginning of this whole series... summer 1994. Although I am in my studio in the mountains, I am dreaming of the beach and find the silliest wooden shaped dowels in a local general store and I glue them all around the border of a small canvas. The center is primed, then shellacked, and pencil gridded ...very pure. I paint the dowels with very bright seashore colors... colors I would never use in a serious painting. I then paint the brightest sunniest white I can find onto the wide border letting the brush hit the sides and tops of the dowels and liking the white smears I am accidentally making on the neatly painted wooden pieces ... and then to finish, I defiantly, trespassingly paint lazy white lines over the pure gridded center and into the border area before I stick this total anomaly away for the next five years because it is so different than anything I have been working on or have ever worked on... in fact I had been working on mourning paintings for nearly two years before and then three after. I call it - with my tongue in my cheek - "Summer Painter".

When I stop to think about it, I've been painting almost nonstop for 35 years. My newest body of work, done over the last three years, has been... I want to use the words pure and magic with all of the meanings that the words 'pure' and 'magic' imply. It seemed to me that in order to go forward, I had to also push backward hard. To again embrace ideas that were at the very foundation of all of my thinking about painting - about structure, about application, about meaning, about materials. I am still seeking clarity, a purity, an essence, but have never been willing to sacrifice the ritual, the need for the deep, the rich, the thick, the dark - the wild wake of the brush and the often organic application of materials - and always working consciously to be in control and out....

Making circles with high ridged edges out of paper maché and slapping white primer paint over the raised areas. Then mixing herbs in a pot with glue and pouring the mixture into the crater created by the ridges and letting it all dry. Finding four large wooden balls and gluing them right in the middle of these pools of herbs and pouring paint over the top of the balls so that it drips into the pools as it covers the balls. Running a large soft black oil stick into the hard ridges of the raised surface so that the color and texture is rich and dark... leaving a very pure and clear middle area of the canvas so that simple thin paint lines of permanent green and brilliant yellow extra pale not only run across this painting but up over top of some of the black ridges and even over the sides and tops of some of the wooden shiny eggplant colored balls... a few tiny flowers... just a few splashes of herbs and only 2 white areas which look wonderful against the raw rabbit skinned glued linen.

Then making courbet green and carbon black ridged paper maché mandelas over and over and over and over with deep orange colored glue, filling each circle and pouring more glue and more herbs into the cavities, some of which have pieces of burlap or silk in them, then crushing alizarin colored oil stick into the centers of the mandelas and the whole configuration is sitting on a golden yellow field with thick yellow grid lines surrounding the circles - all coming together like a drum beat or a deep chant I can hear....

Going to a flea market in Santa Fe and getting completely turned on by deep blue Russian glass beads and very light-blue opaque glass colored beads and having no idea what I might do with these beads - saving them -and then finding small plastic dark green beads on Canal Street in the bins in the plastics store. Creating a deep center gridded center field using light gray and green pastel lines and erasing them over and over into the unbleached rabbit skinned glued canvas to get the depth - and building a border of paper maché around the pure field - gluing the plastic beads all around onto the border of the painting and taking cadmium green pale and cadmium lemon oil sticks and grinding them into the hard ridges of the outer field, making sure to leave the green plastic beads and the little pools around the beads showing and thinking how absolutely luminous the yellow green colors are - like crushed green light - and then running the black painted lines of the grid into the crushed green field. How good that felt.

And to continue with the idea of jewels bedecking a grid painting... gluing little wooden pedestals around the rim of the painting... messily painting these small wooden spools over and over as if they were the waterfront pilings that I saw in Provincetown that are painted over and over year after year until they develop crusts of paint on top and splashes of colors down the sides with pools of paint at the base... and then setting my Russian glass beads atop these painted pedestals and creating a very pure white field in the center of this painting and drawing a tentative grid with blue pastels and running glue into it so it becomes liquid and then pulling rounded rope-like grid lines of yellow and deeper yellow over the smooth white field... keeping these lines going into the outside turquoise blue field created for the glass bead pedestal area.

A long, very horizontal canvas that will use the light blue beads atop a set of white painted dowels of different heights - stations - points - beats - surrounded by white ghostlike pools of paint set in a brilliant blue field - no explanation necessary or even possible -and needing 27 beads in all and finding out that is exactly how many I had bought at the flea market - magic - and then running the yellow and white and blue lines back and forth and over and over as they come out of the tube almost on their own and sometimes stop and start and fall and dip and then straighten out again just to get to the end of the long canvas, crossing and crossing still further into the turquoise border...the many beautiful blues that remind me of the sea and the yellow... the sun... the lines a language that is speaking and is in and out of my control as it makes its journey across the middle of the painting and I frame the whole picture with a very thin bright red line because....

Going to Woodstock to paint last summer and feeling so strongly the ghost of my mother in the studio that I start working on a completely different painting than I had planned. Writing "spring is an issue of blood" across the painting - T.S. Eliot's words from his play "Family Reunion"- because I have always felt that "April is the cruelest month"... has been my whole life... in the spring, the month I was born ... when I always had my little and bigger nervous breakdowns and even a miscarriage and then on the bottom of the painting writing his words again "Do the dead want to return?" because surely my mother has been in my studio all summer haunting me. Then painting out most of those words because they appear too strong and they overwhelm the painting - the painting which is pulsating and undulating on its own without those words - except "THE DEAD" because I just can't let go of that one word.

Reading James Joyce's play "The Exiles" and then his own words in the back of the book describing Bertha, saying, "She is the earth, dark, formless, mother, made beautiful by the moonlit night, darkly conscious of her instincts." And having those words resonate so deeply inside of me that I have to write them across the painting I am working on - because that very painting that very day has moons and moonlight and flowers and breasts and darkness and even fear - all over it....

Then looking in the bedroom mirror one day and seeing reflected in the mirror my small 1970 stroke painting that is hanging over our bed - next to a vase of beautiful deep/red/purplish flowers that is on the dresser next to the mirror and creating a dyptich of its own and being so taken with the image that I am not able to give up the idea of combining the strokes and the flowers into one painting - not even sure if it works but in so many ways it is what I am about - the clear precise analytical over- the- top flower field expressionist.

Having a plan, a very well thought out idea, even a carefully drawn image for a painting all ready and then the painting begins to take me over and goes where it wants to go - and I let it because I know that a ritual is going on - that the forms in the middle of the pools of herbs are primal. I didn't invent those configurations, but I use them when I have to - and Kali's angry tongue appears all over the border of the painting along with deep red cherry lines and then tiny silk rags are placed onto red marks so that the paint becomes blood and seeps into the material and somehow I finally know that this painting has become a ritual for my daughter Molly and her friends Marni and Becky and Felix and Orlando and Georgio and all her other friends whom I love and worry about.

A sunflower field, again, this time in winter - after it is done with blooming and way beyond that even - with rusts and oranges and herbs and turquoise and pale lemon yellow rectangles that create another rhythm besides that of the death of the flowers - it is a very quiet painting and I love it - it seems very sad and I think of the words ancient tears....

JOAN SNYDER *NEW YORK, 2001*

SUMMER PAINTER, 1994
Oil, acrylic, paper maché, and wooden dowels on linen
17 x 20 inches

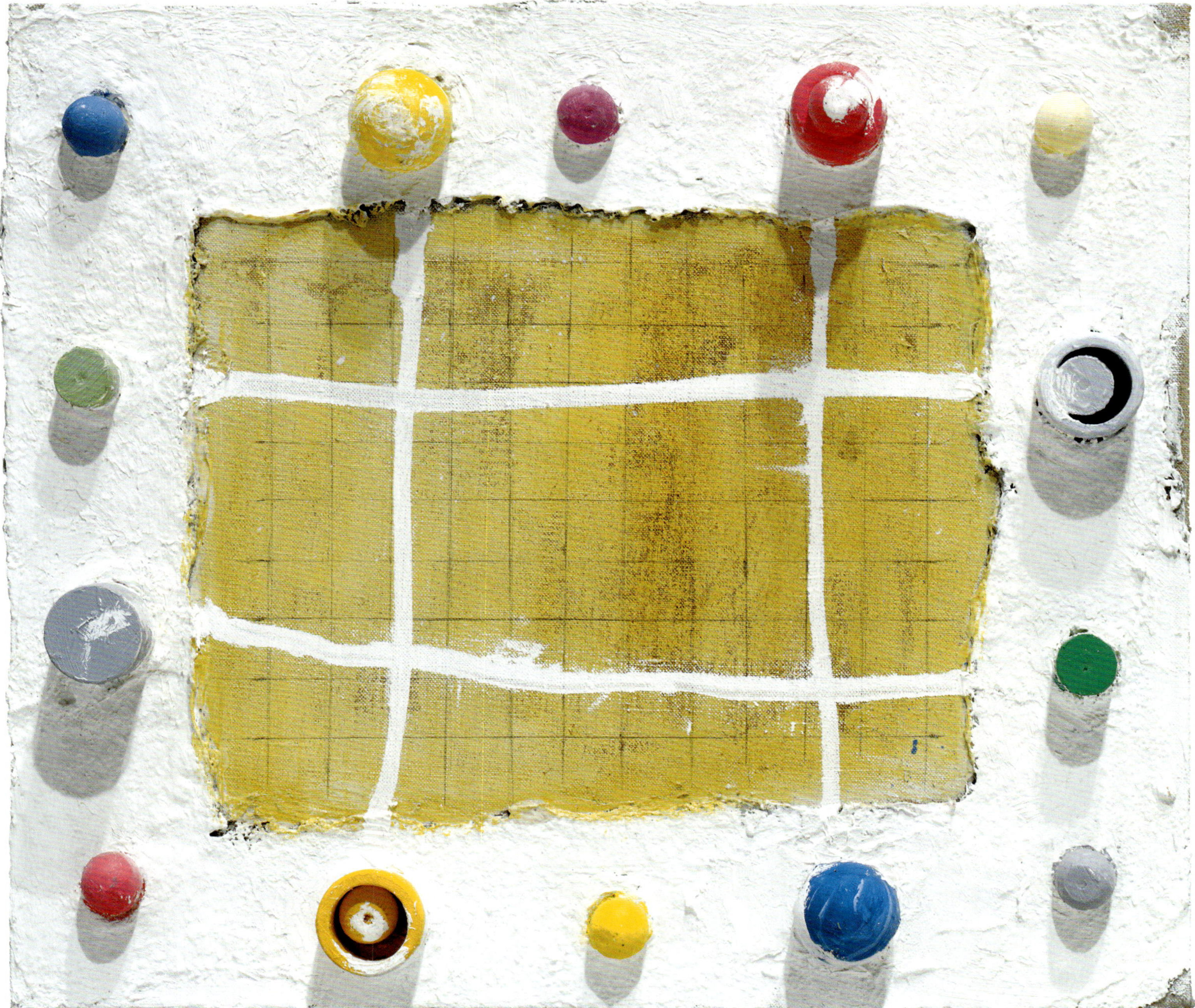

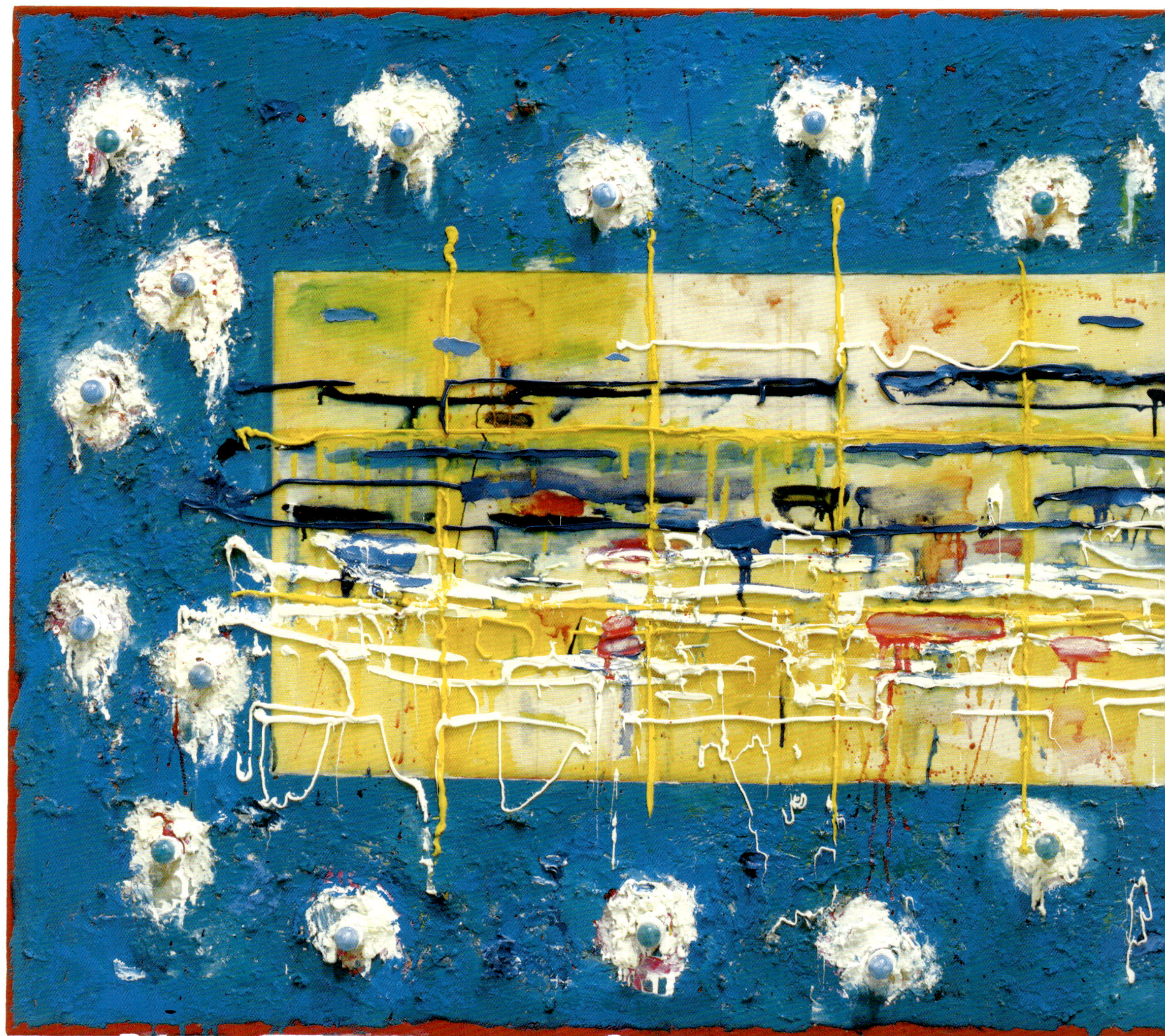

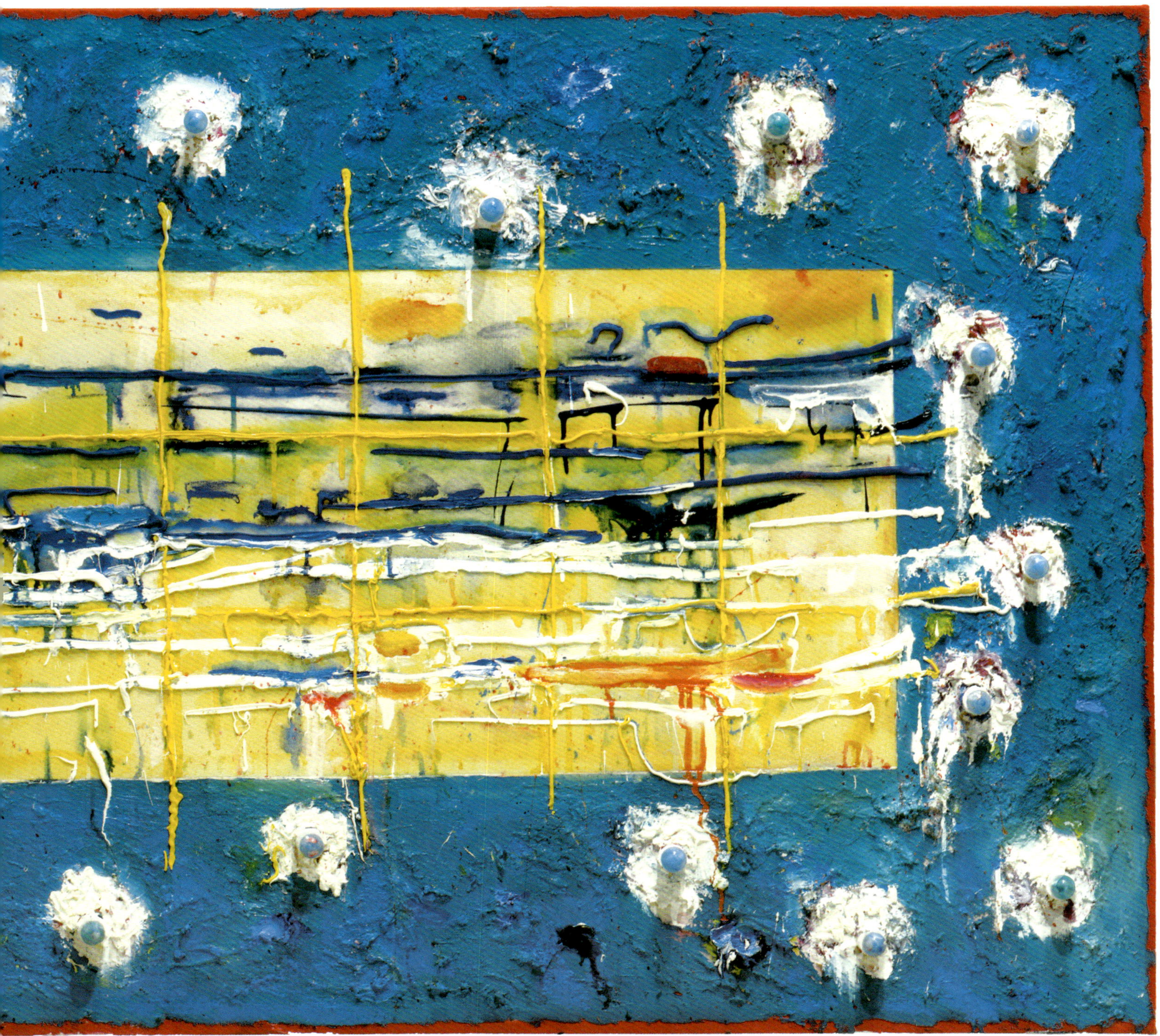

CRUSHED GREEN LIGHT, 1998
Oil, acrylic, pastel, paper maché, charcoal
wooden dowels, and plastic beads, on canvas
40 x 40 inches

PREVIOUS PAGE:
LANGUAGE OF THE SEA, 1999
Oil, acrylic, paper maché, wooden dowels,
and glass beads on canvas
39 x 90 inches

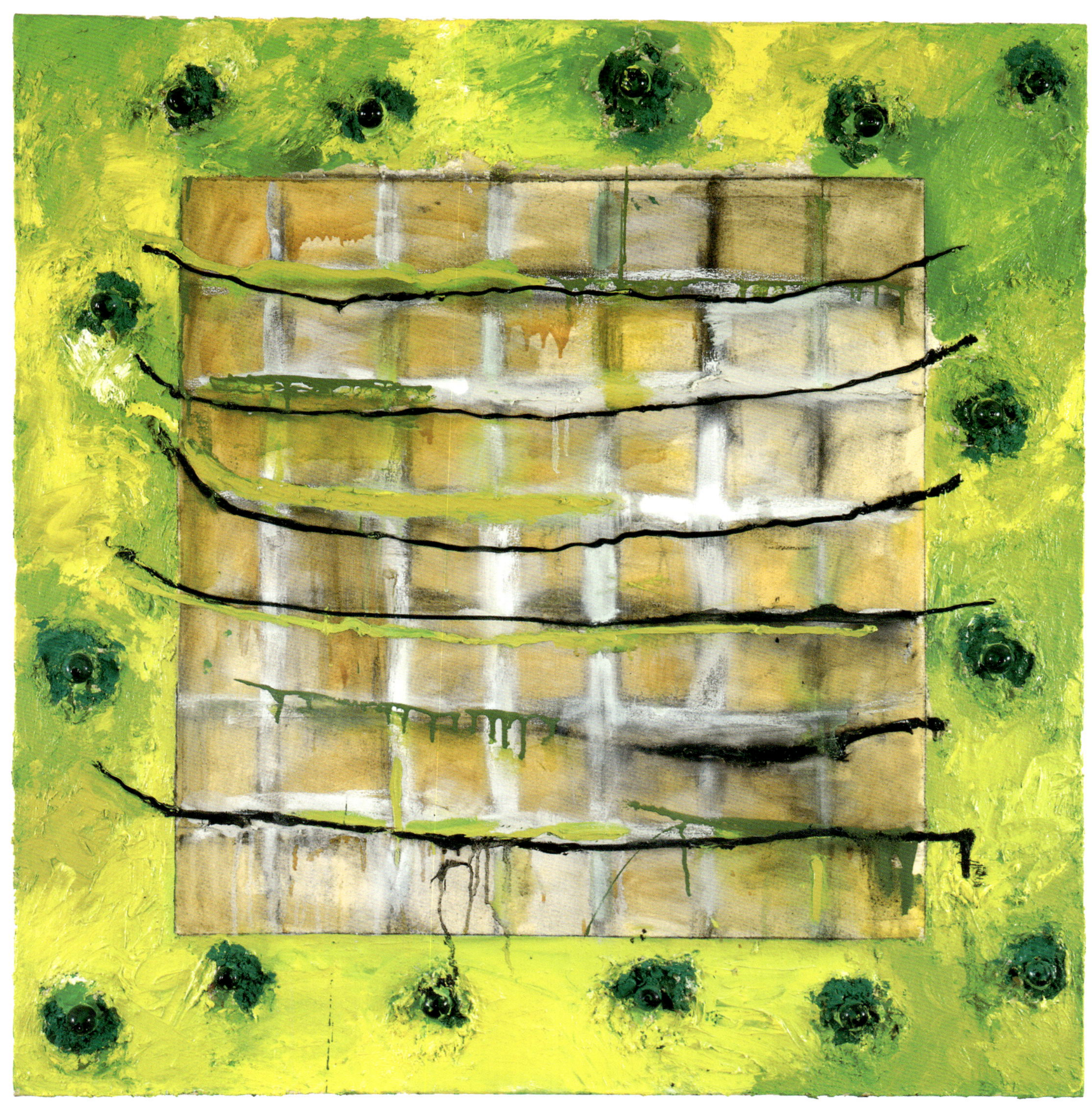

SUNTOON BLUES, 1998
Oil, acrylic, paper maché, wooden dowels,
and glass beads on canvas
32 1/2 x 46 inches

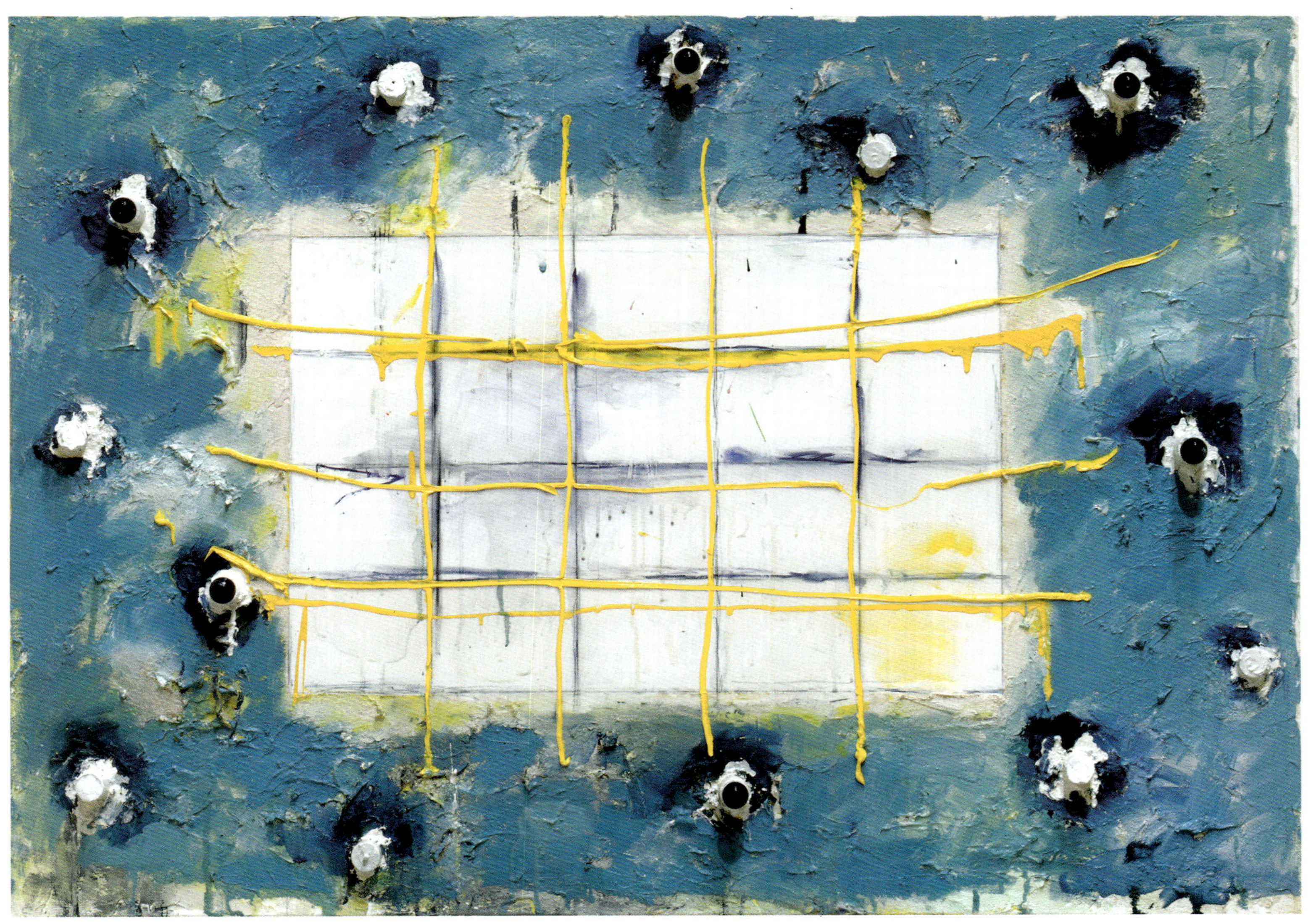

THE ESSENCE, 2000
Oil, acrylic, paper maché, herbs, and wooden balls on linen mounted on wood
36 x 48 inches

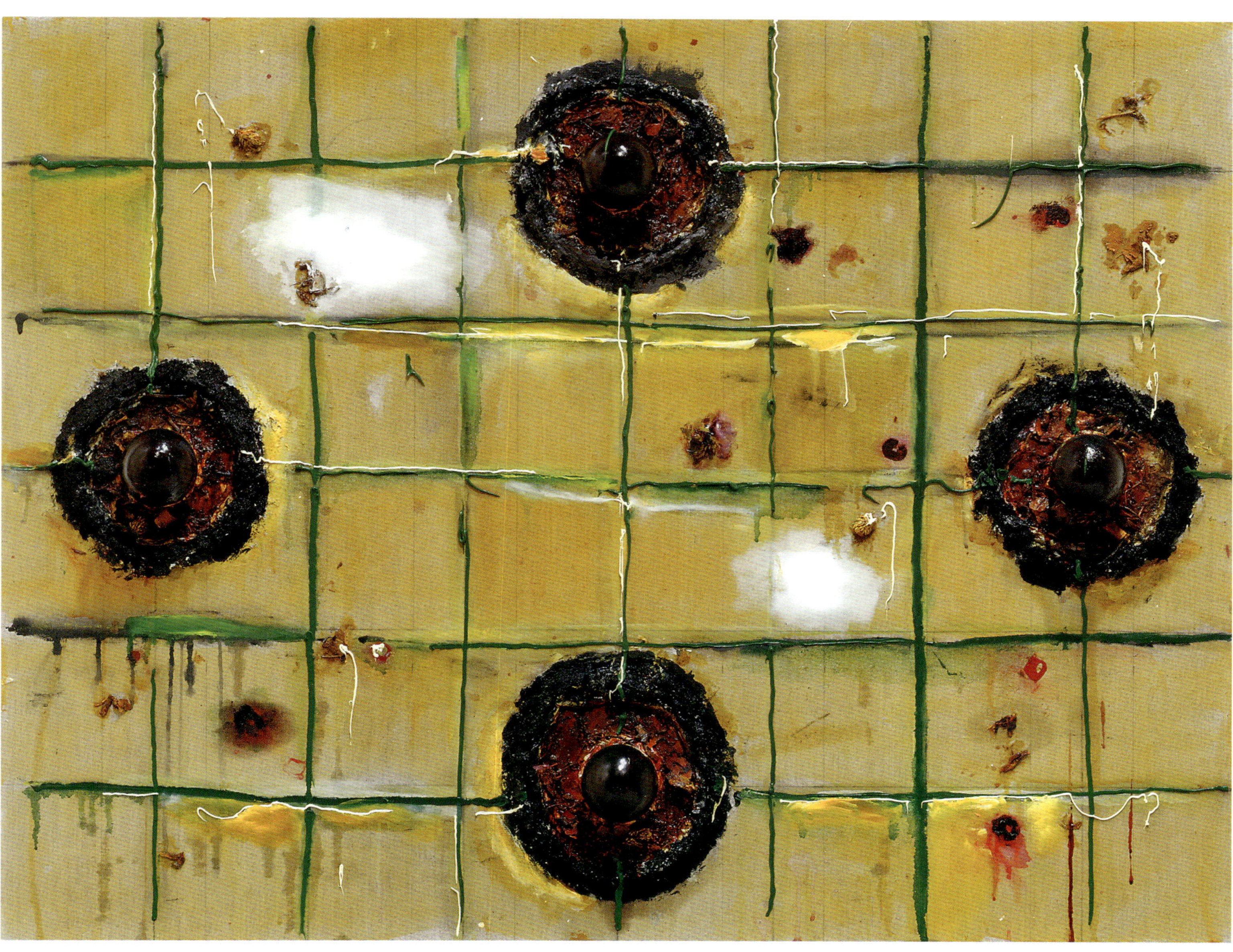

ROUGH CHANT, 2000
Oil, acrylic, paper maché, cloth, and
herbs on canvas
72 x 78 inches

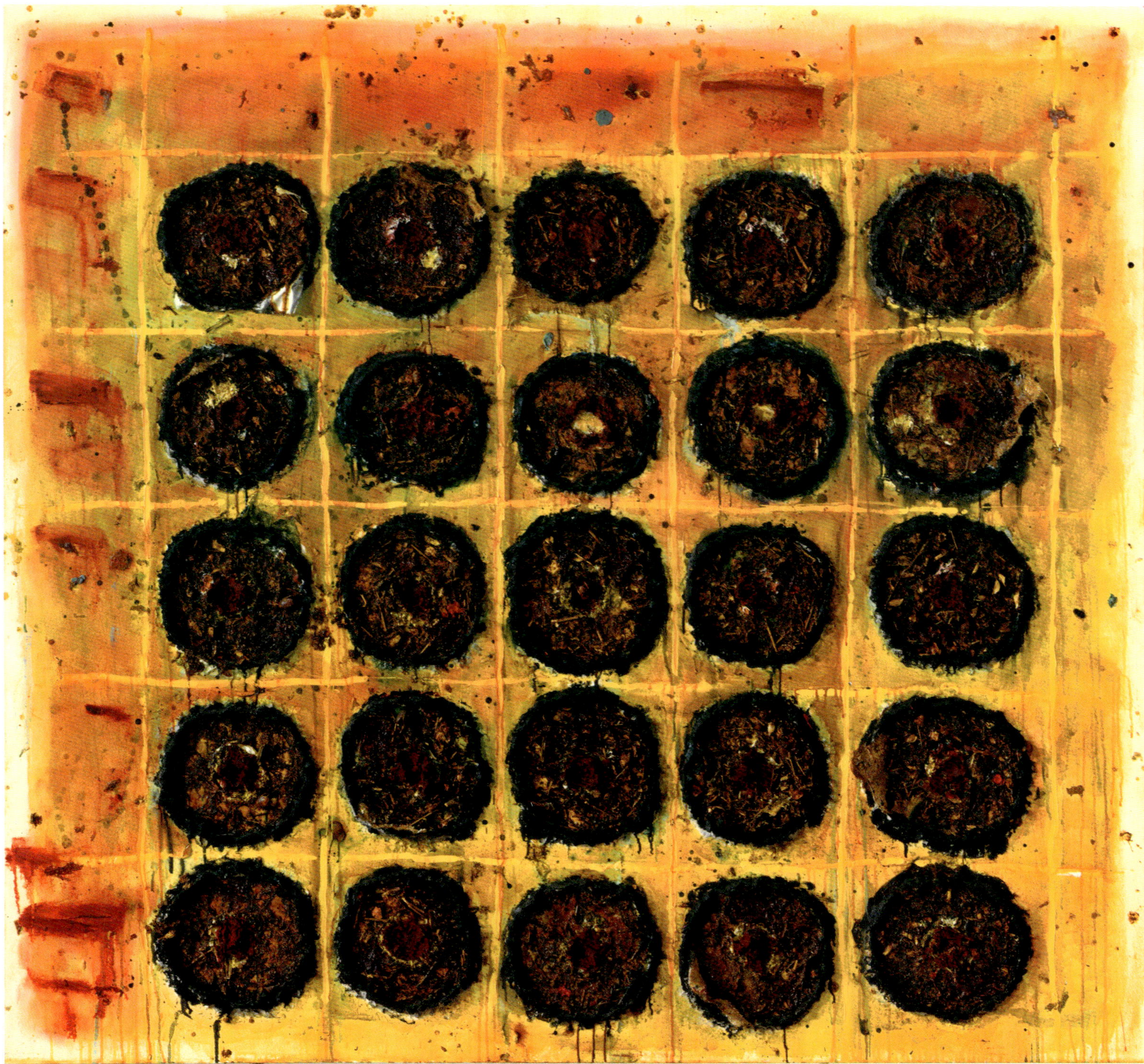

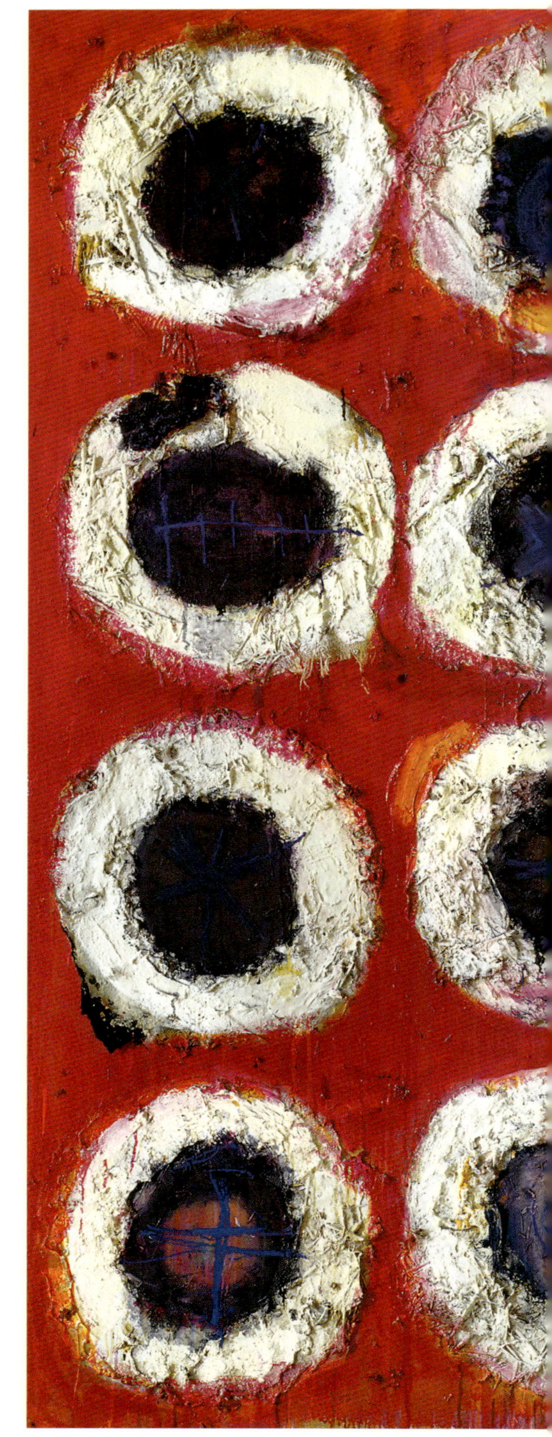

TO BEAR ALL THINGS, 2001
Oil, acrylic, paper maché, silk,
burlap, and herbs on linen
78 x 120 inches

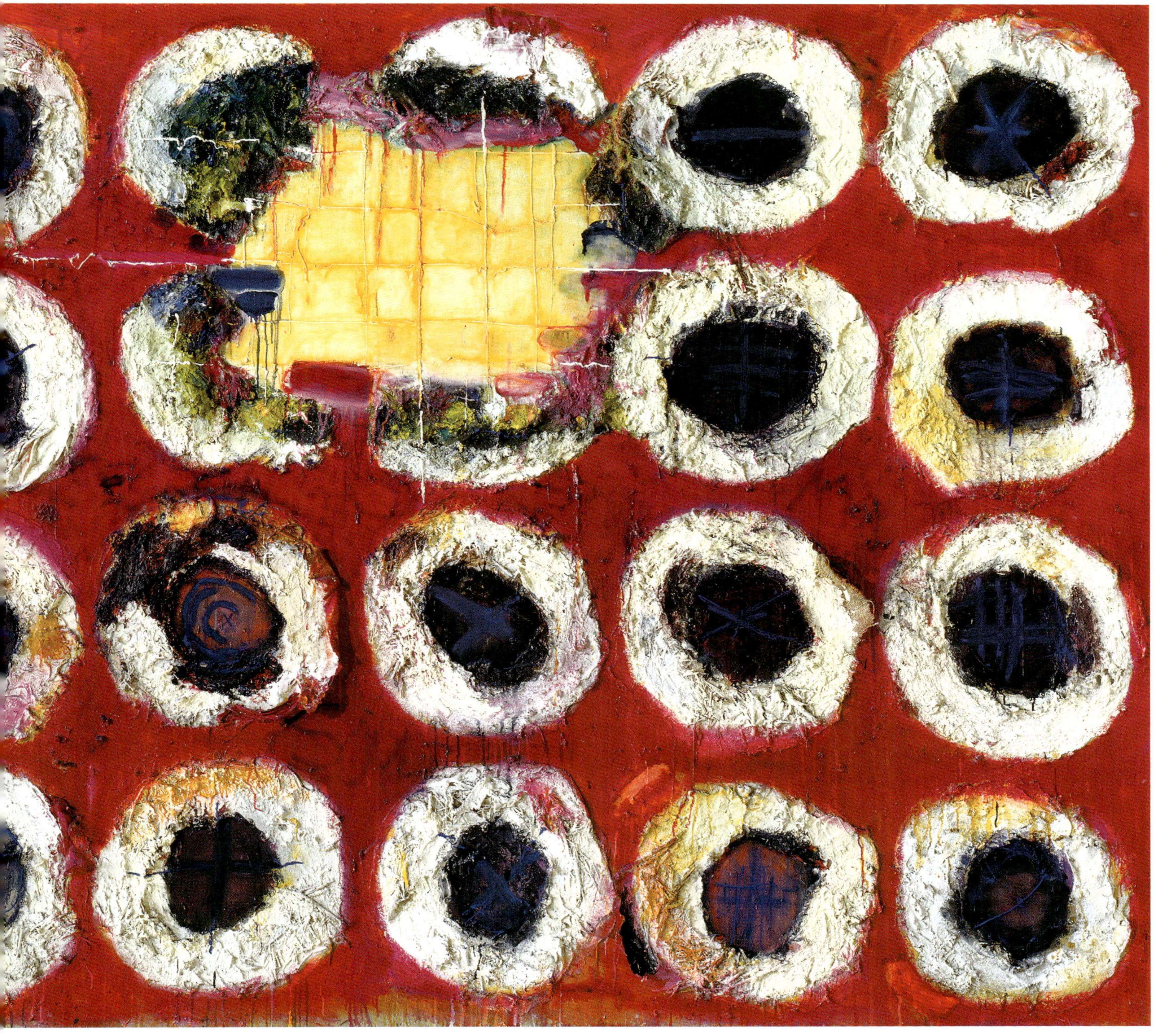

LEMON YELLOW FIELD, 2001
Oil, acrylic, paper maché,
and herbs on linen on board
36 x 48 inches

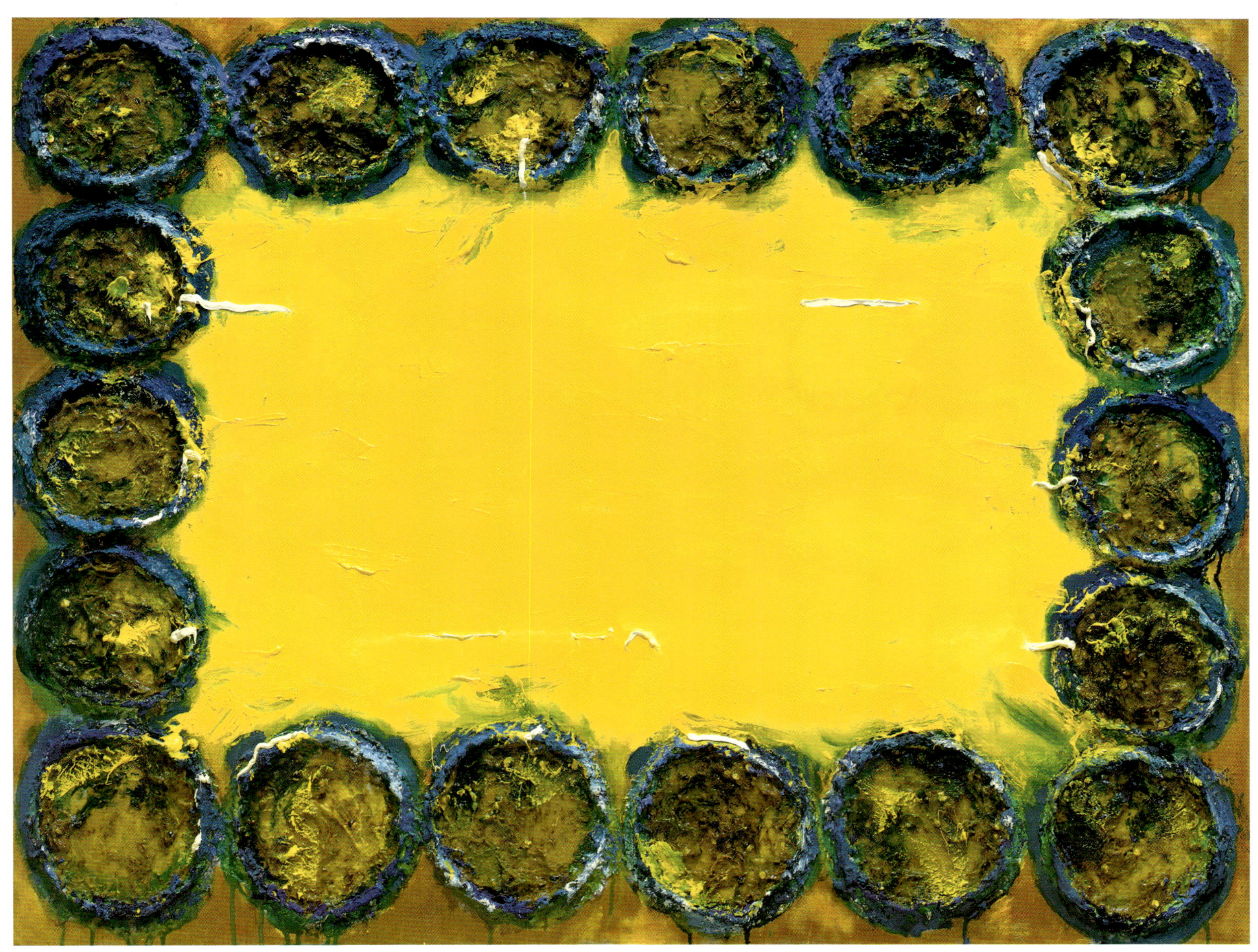

VOYAGE, 2000
Oil, acrylic, paper maché, burlap,
velvet, and herbs on canvas
72 x 78 inches

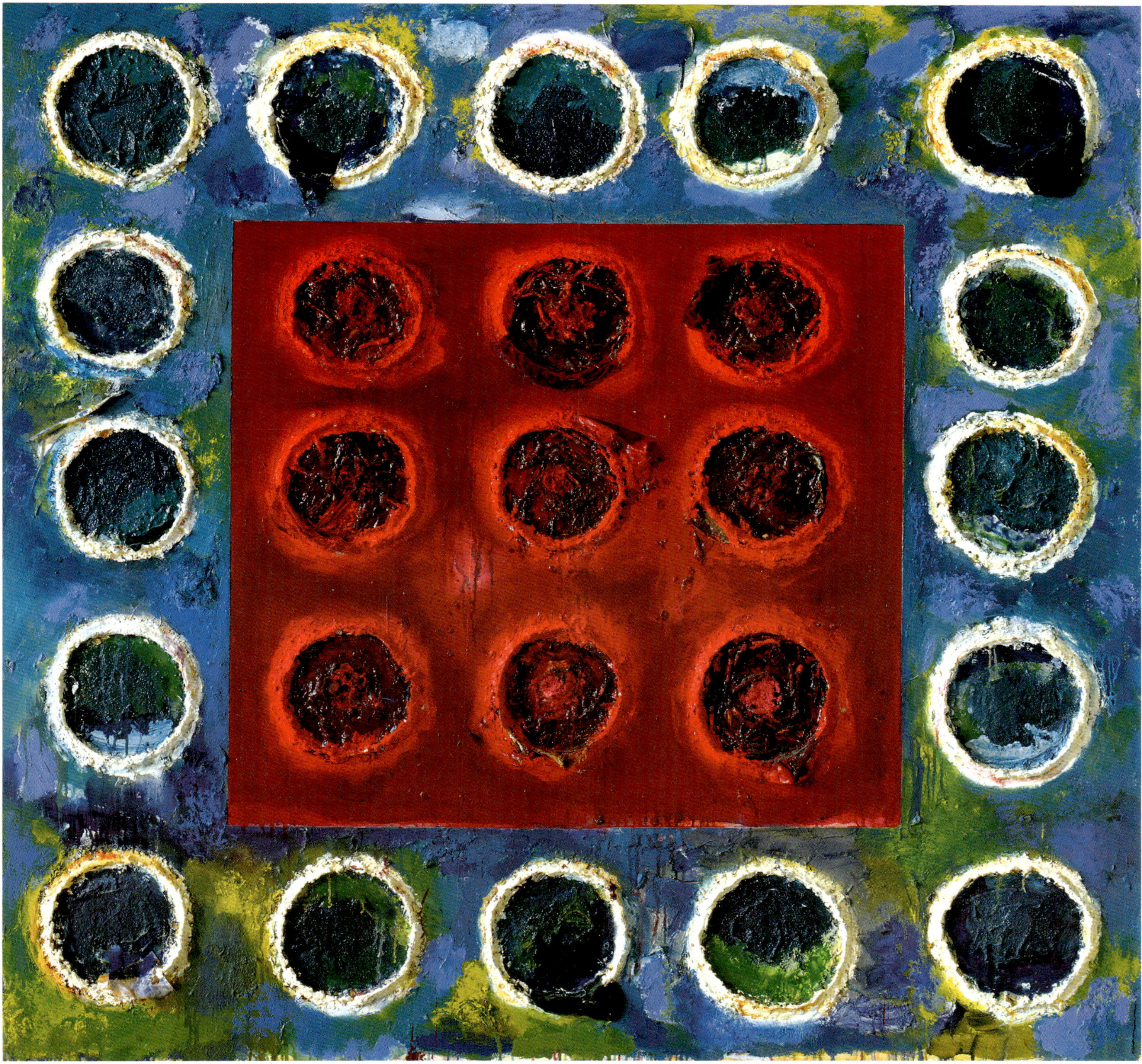

RITUAL, 2001
Oil, acrylic, paper maché,
burlap, and herbs on linen
72 x 84 inches

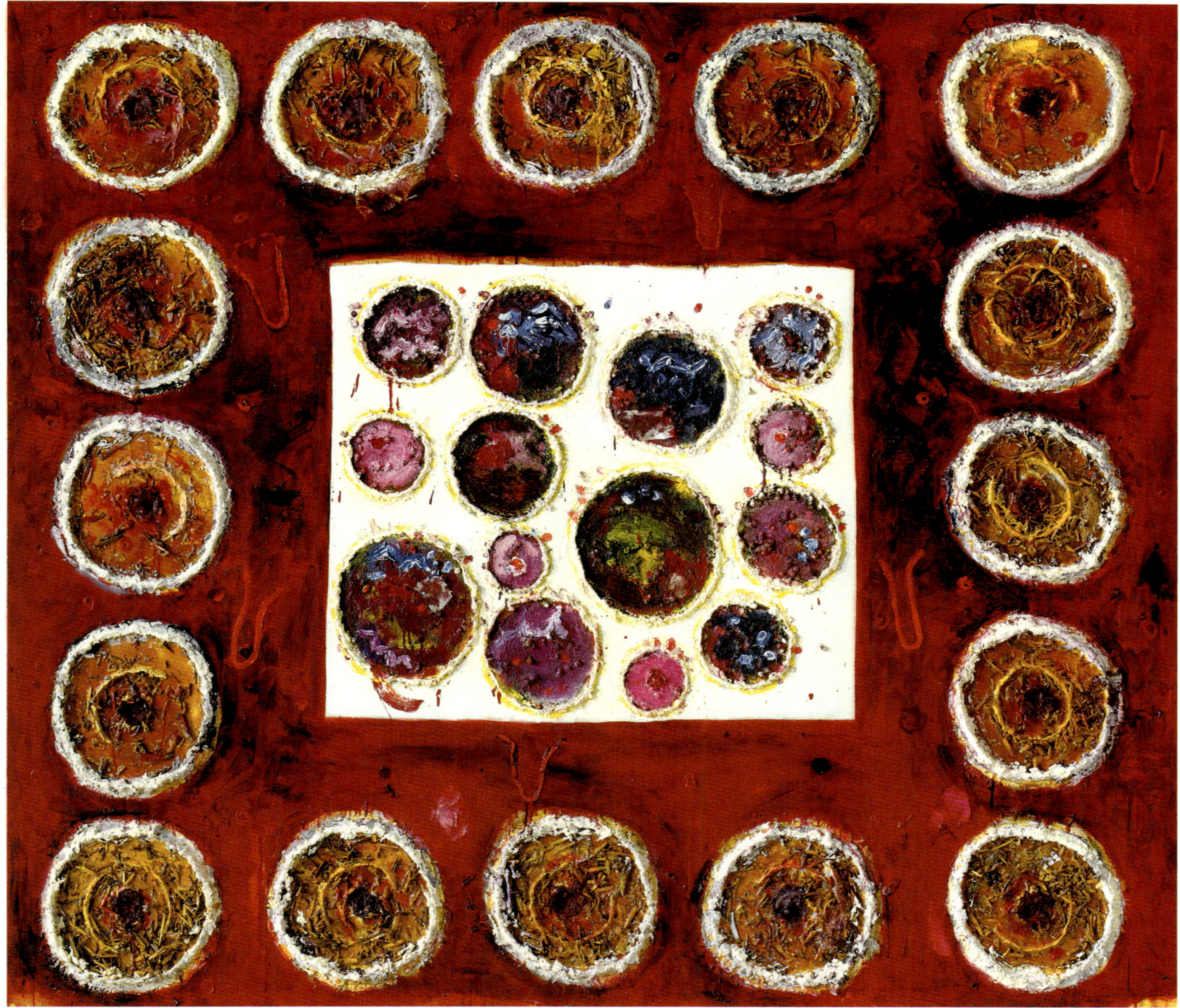

BLUE/MOONS, 2000
Oil, acrylic, paper maché, silk, burlap,
and herbs on canvas on board
54 x 66 inches

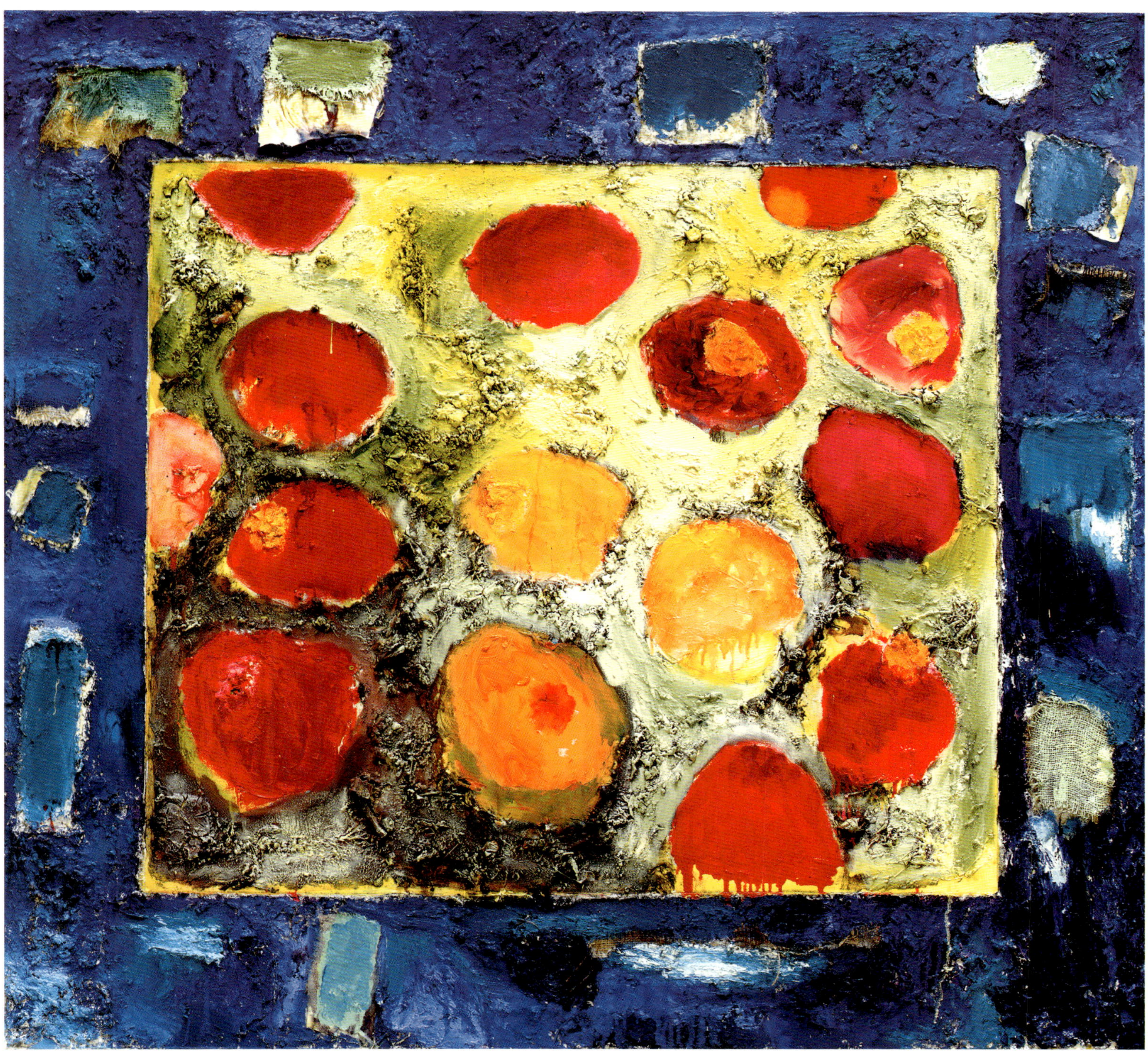

SHE IS THE EARTH, 2000
Oil, acrylic, paper maché, and
herbs on wood panels
72 x 96 inches

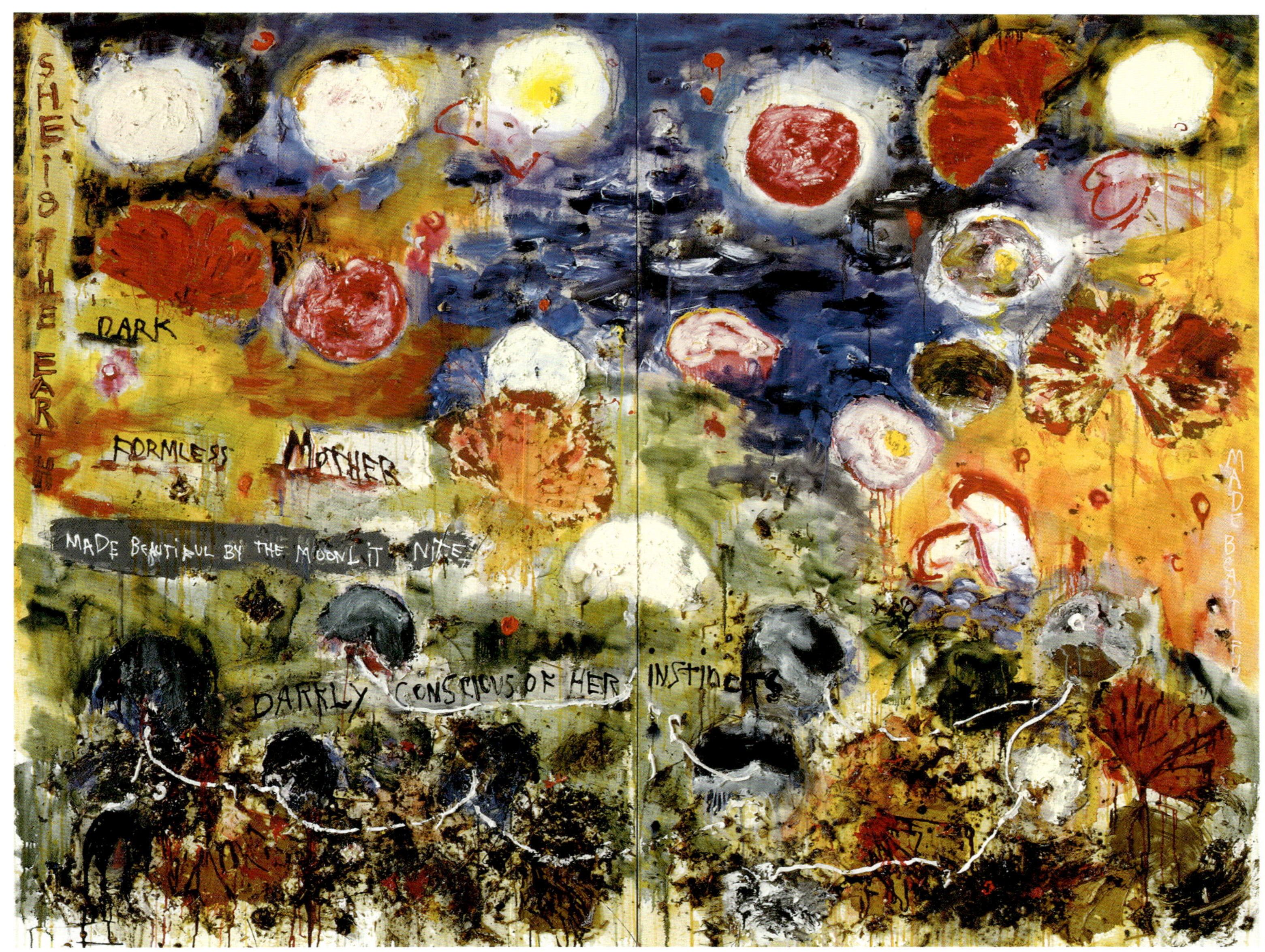
SHE IS THE EARTH
DARK
FORMLESS
MOTHER
MADE BEAUTIFUL BY THE MOONLIT NITE
DARKLY CONSCIOUS OF HER INSTINCTS
MADE BEAUTIFUL

GHOSTS, 2000
Oil, acrylic, paper maché, silk,
burlap, and straw on canvas
72 x 96 inches

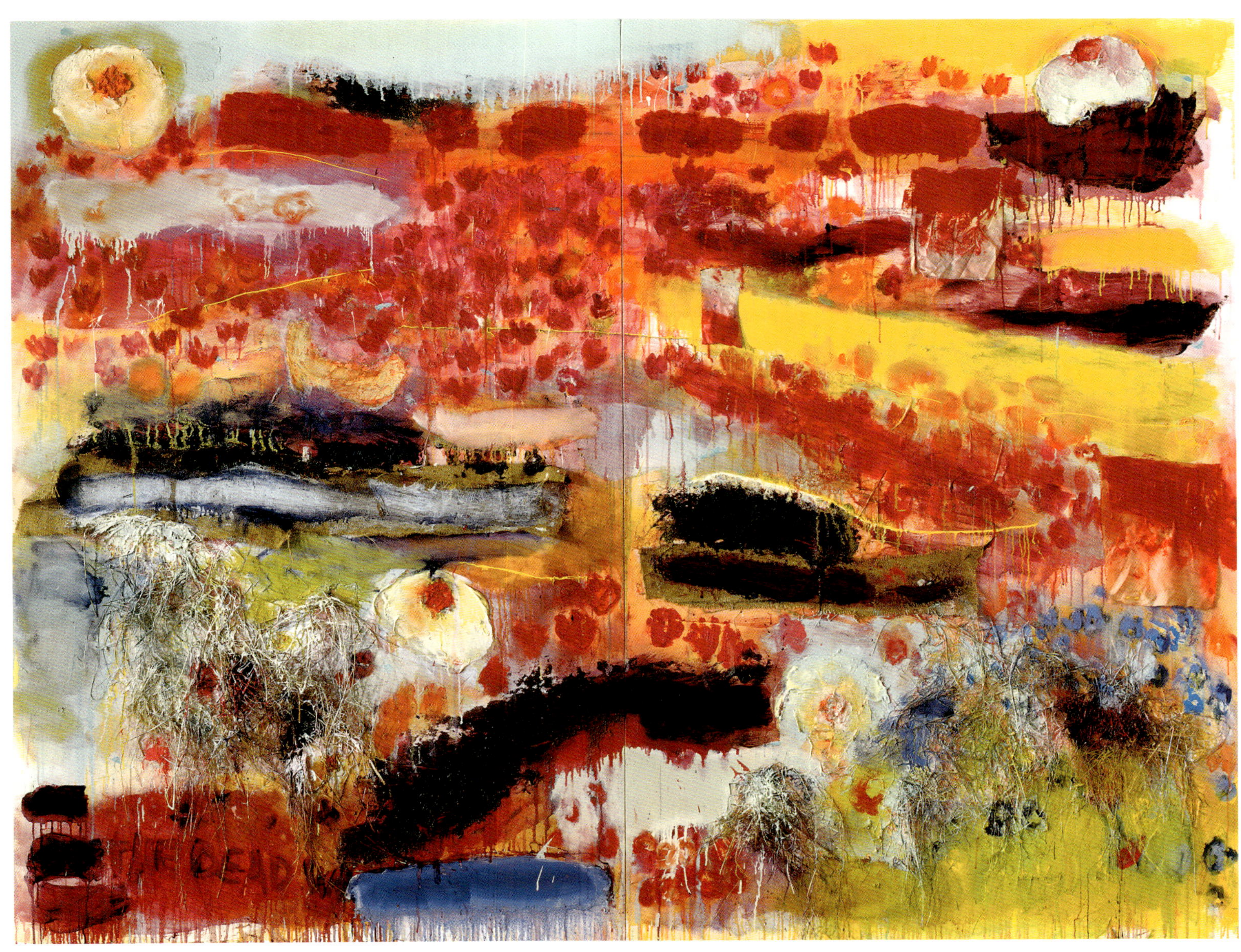

AND ALWAYS SEARCHING FOR BEAUTY, 2001
Oil, acrylic, paper maché,
and herbs on linen
78 x 102 inches

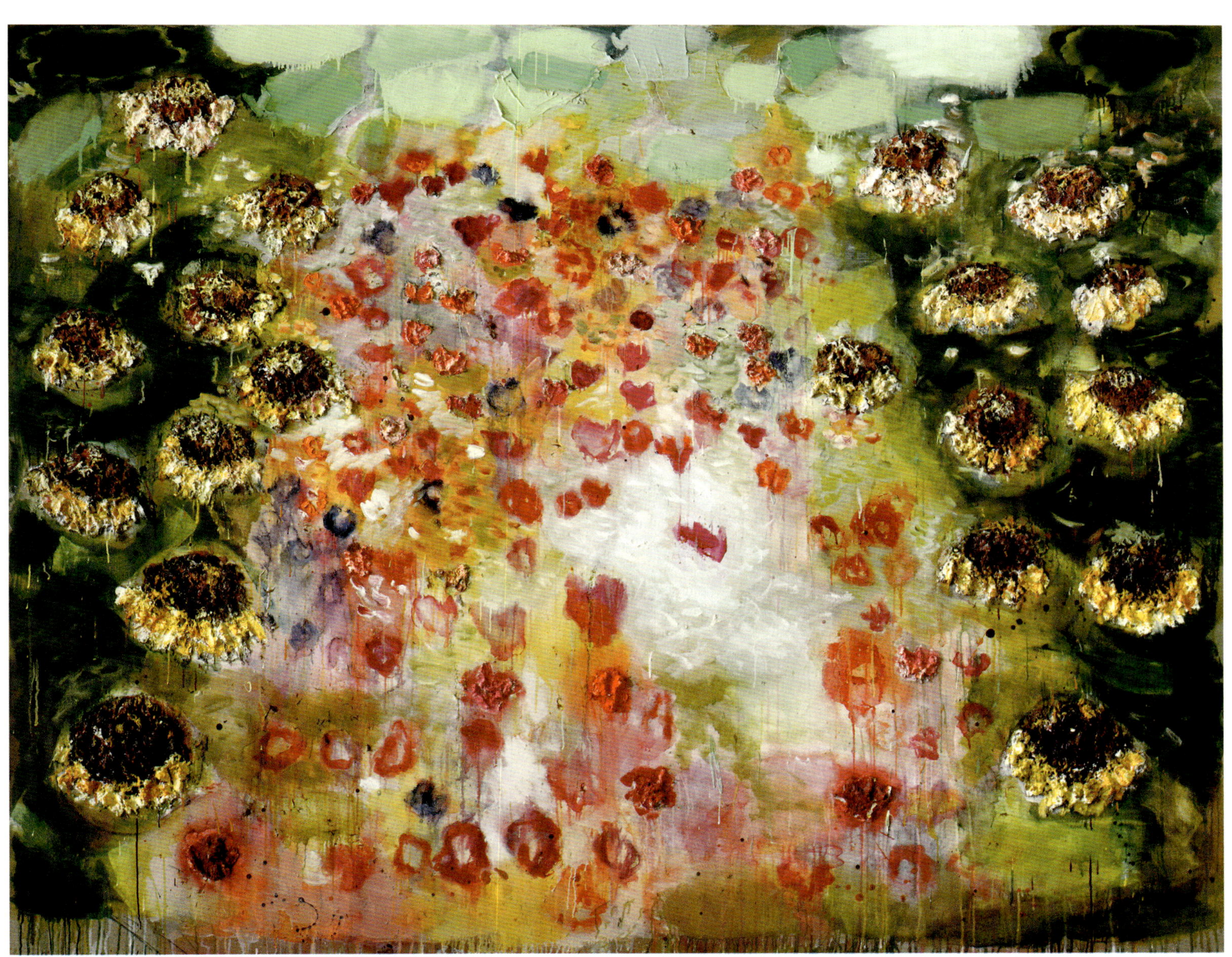

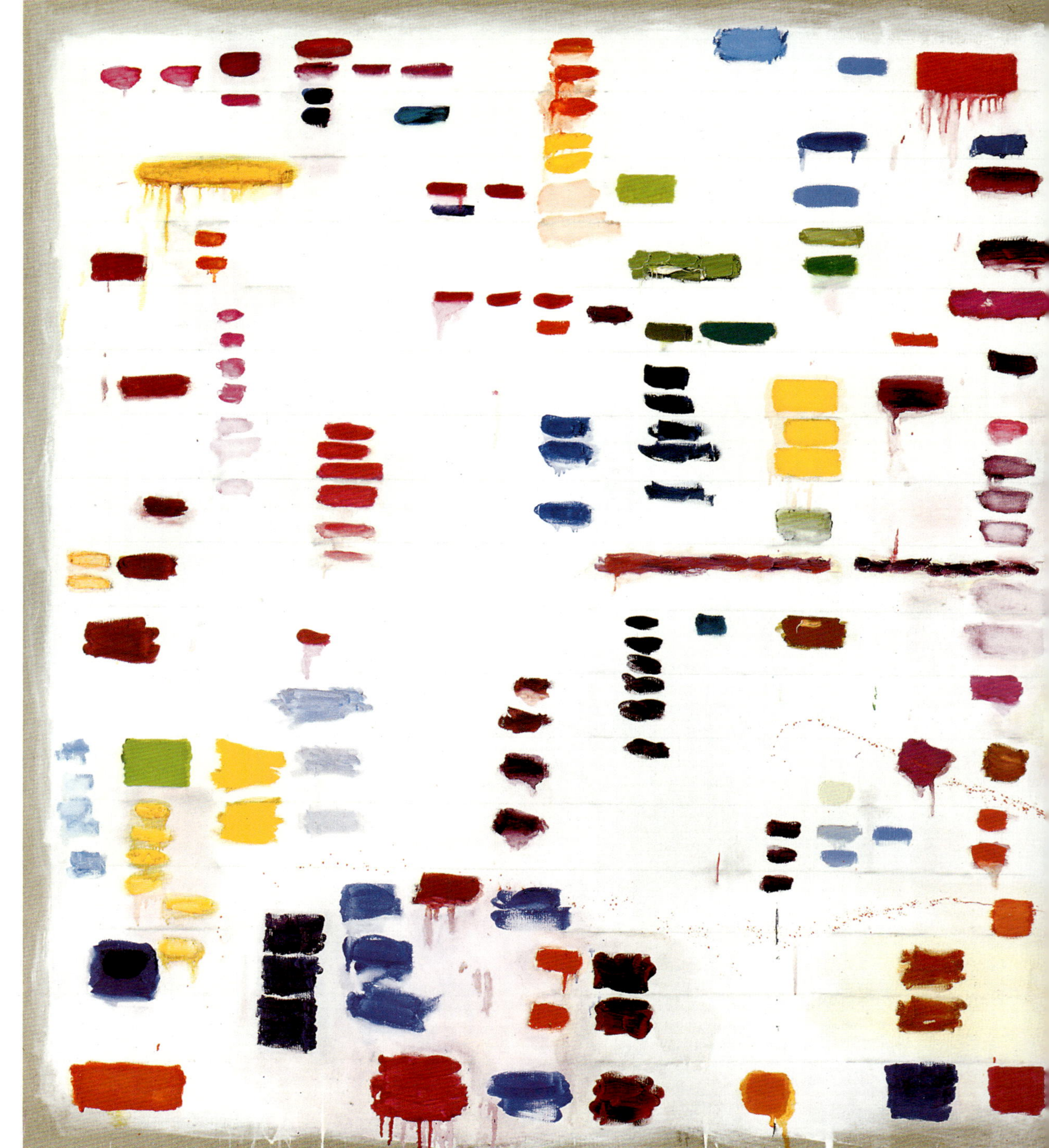

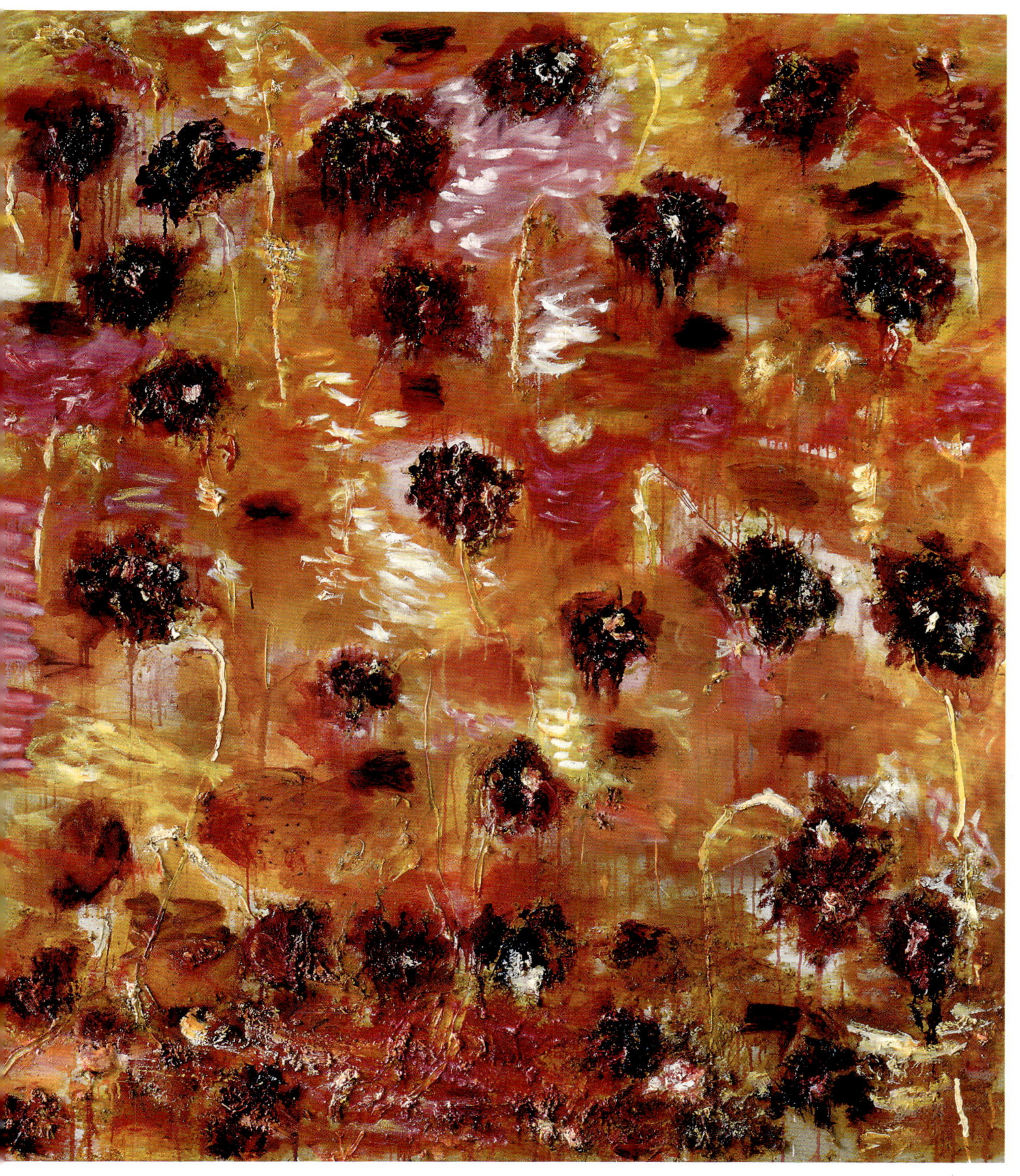

To be private
Not to be private
To run
Not to run
My soul
How do you paint a soul

J.S. 1970

LACRYMAE ANTIGUA (Ancient Tears), 2000
Oil, acrylic, cloth, mud,
and herbs on canvas
72 x 78 inches

PREVIOUS PAGE
PRIMARY FIELDS (Diptych), 2001
Oil, acrylic, and herbs on linen
72 x 132 inches

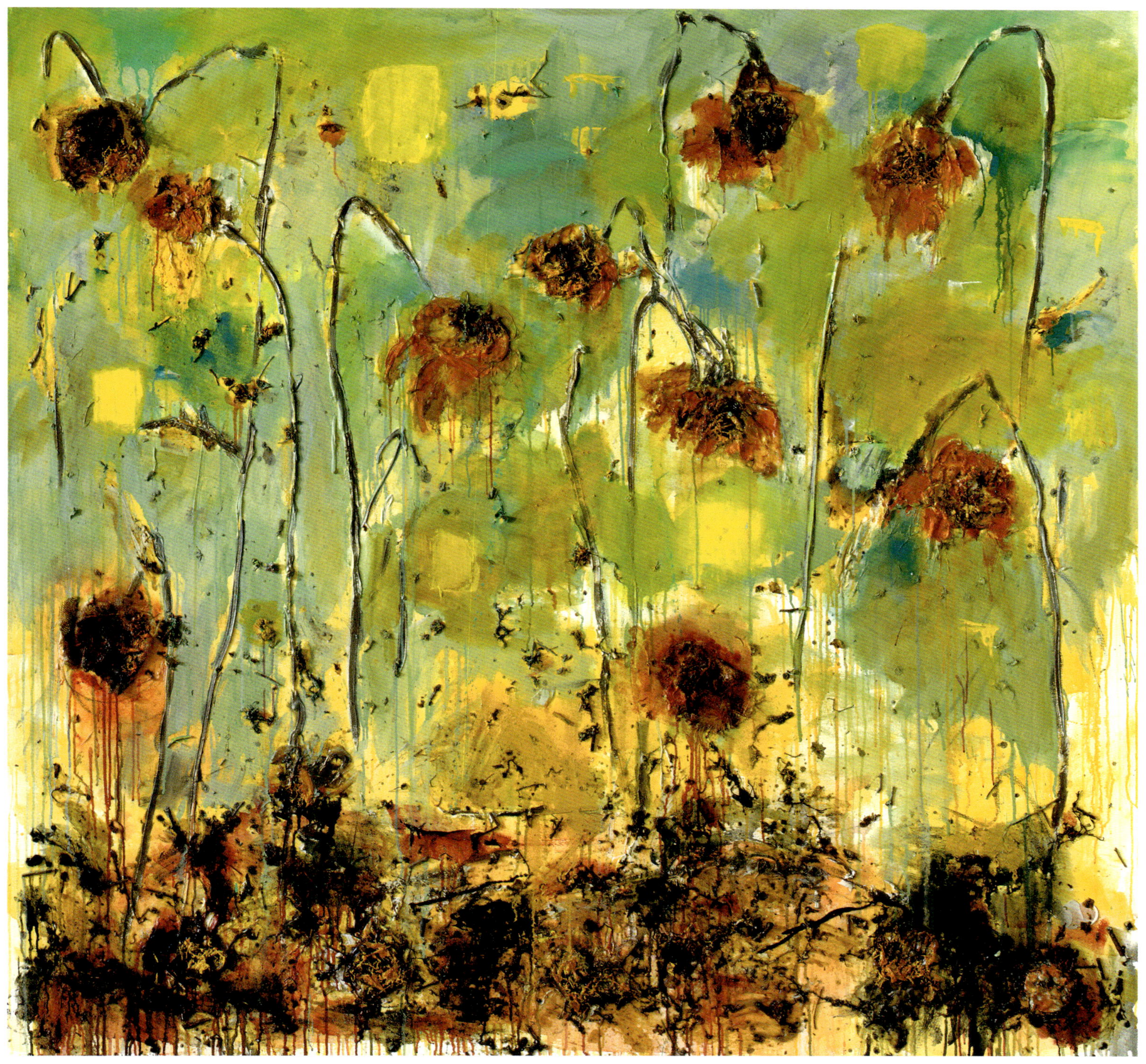

BIOGRAPHY

1940 Born, Highland Park, New Jersey, April 16th

1962 B.A., Douglass College, New Brunswick, New Jersey

1966 M.F.A., Rutgers, The State University of New Jersey, New Brunswick

Lives and works in Brooklyn and Woodstock, New York

SOLO EXHIBITIONS

1966 Douglass College, Rutgers, The State University of New Jersey, New Brunswick, *Paintings, Sculpture: Master of Fine Arts Thesis Exhibition* (April 13 – 25)

1967 Little Gallery, New Brunswick, NJ

1970 Paley & Lowe, New York, *Three Paintings* (December)

1971 Michael Walls Gallery, San Francisco, *Joan Snyder New Paintings* (August 11 – September 4)

Paley & Lowe, New York, *Paintings*

Bykert Gallery, New York

1972 Parker Street 470 Gallery, Boston, *Joan Snyder* (April 14 – May 6)

1973 Paley & Lowe, New York, *Paintings* (April 21 – May 16)

1975 Carl Solway Gallery, New York, *Joan Snyder: New Work, 1974-75* (February 6 – March 13)

1976 Reed College, Portland, *Joan Snyder: Works on Paper 1973-75* (March 27 – April 25)

Mabel Smith Douglass Library, Douglass College, Rutgers, The State University of New Jersey, New Brunswick, *Joan Snyder* (April 19 – May 14)

Portland Center for the Visual Arts, Portland, *Joan Snyder Recent Paintings* (May 6 – June 1)

Los Angeles Institute of Contemporary Art, Los Angeles (August 10 – September 10)

Broxton Gallery, Los Angeles

1977 Wake Forest University, Winston-Salem, NC, *Joan Snyder* (April 18 – May 13)

1978 Neuberger Museum of Art, Purchase College, State University of New York, Purchase, *Joan Snyder: Seven Years of Work* (January 17 – March 4)

Hamilton Gallery, New York, *Joan Snyder New Work* (February 18 – March 25)

1979 Hamilton Gallery, New York, *New Paintings*

Women's Art Registry of Minnesota, Minneapolis, *A Woman's Collective Art Space*

Santa Barbara Contemporary Arts Forum, Santa Barbara, CA, *Joan Snyder at W.A.R.M. A Women's Collective Art Space* (May 7 – June 17) (exhibition traveled to San Francisco Art Institute, San Francisco; Grand Rapids Art Museum, Grand Rapids; The Renaissance Society at the University of Chicago, Chicago; Anderson Gallery, Virginia Commonwealth University, Richmond)

1981 Matrix Gallery, Wadsworth Athenaeum, Hartford, CT, *Resurrection and Studies*

Nielsen Gallery, Boston, *Joan Snyder Works on Paper: Studies for F.M.S.W.N.L.*

1982 Hamilton Gallery, New York, *New Work*

1983 Nielsen Gallery, Boston

1985 Hirschl & Adler Modern, New York

1986 Nielsen Gallery, Boston

1988 Compass Rose Gallery, Chicago, *Joan Snyder: Cantatas and Requiems*

Hirschl & Adler Modern, New York

1988-89 Santa Barbara Contemporary Arts Forum, Santa Barbara, CA, *Joan Snyder Collects Joan Snyder* (exhibition traveled to Brown University, Providence; State University of New York, Stony Brook; De Saisset Museum, Santa Clara University, Santa Clara, CA (September 14 – October 29, 1989)

1989 Compass Rose Gallery, Chicago, *New Painting by Joan Snyder* (November – December)

1990 Hirschl & Adler Modern, New York, *Joan Snyder* (February 3 – 28)

Victoria Munroe Gallery, New York, *Monotype Project 1988-1989* (October 4 – November 3)

1991 Ann Jaffe Gallery, Miami Beach, *Joan Snyder* (January 25 – February 16)

Nielsen Gallery, Boston (opened October 11)

1992 Hirschl & Adler Modern, New York, *Joan Snyder*

1993 Rena Bransten Gallery, San Francisco, *Joan Snyder* (May 13 – June 12)

Fine Arts Work Center, Provincetown, MA, *Monoprints for AIDS Portfolio* (opened September 24)

1993-94 Allentown Art Museum, Allentown, PA, *Joan Snyder: Works with Paper* (October 8, 1993 – January 2, 1994)

1994 Hirschl & Adler Modern, New York, *Joan Snyder: Works With Paper* (March 5 – April 16) [selections from an exhibition curated by Sarah Anne McNear at the Allentown Art Museum, Allentown, PA]

Nielsen Gallery, Boston, *Joan Snyder Recent Works* (April 9 – May 7)

Rose Art Museum, Brandeis University; Waltham, MA, *Joan Snyder: Painter 1969 to Now* (April 15 – June 5) (exhibition traveled to The Parrish Art Museum, Southampton, NY (July 9 – August 28) [selected "Best Regional Show" by the International Critics Association,1994]

1995 Locks Gallery, Philadelphia, PA, *Joan Snyder New Paintings* (May 5 – June 17)

1996 Quartet Editions, New York, *Joan Snyder, New Monoprints* (March 23 – May 4)

Hirschl & Adler Modern, New York, *Joan Snyder: Paintings 1995-96* (March 30 – May 11)

Jane Voorhees Zimmerli Art Museum, Rutgers, The State University of New Jersey, New Brunswick, *Joan Snyder: New Works on Paper*

1997 Nielsen Gallery, Boston (November)

1998 The Brooklyn Museum of Art, Brooklyn, *Joan Snyder: Working in Brooklyn* (March 6 – June 14)

Hirschl & Adler Modern, New York, *Joan Snyder New Paintings* (April 25 – June 12)

2000 Nielsen Gallery, Boston, *In Times of Great Disorder* (May 13 – June 3)

2000-01 The Philadelphia Museum of Jewish Art, Philadelphia, *Kaddish / Requiem* (December 8, 2000 – April 16, 2001)

2001 Robert Miller Gallery, New York, *Joan Snyder Primary Fields* (April 25 – May 26)

Revolution, Ferndale, MI, *Joan Snyder* (April 28 – May 26)

GROUP EXHIBITIONS

1970 The New Gallery, Cleveland, *Small Works* (opened December 4)

A Clean Well Lighted Place, Austin

Dayton's Gallery 12, Minneapolis

1971 Glauber-Poons Gallery, Amsterdam

Bykert Gallery, New York (February)

Mansfield Fine Arts Museum, Mansfield, OH, *Into the 70s*

Paley & Lowe Gallery, New York, *Joan Snyder, Paintings; Laurence Fink, Photographs* (November 6 – 27)

1972 Whitney Museum of American Art, New York, *1972 Annual Exhibition: Contemporary American Painting* (January 25 – March 19)

Institute of Contemporary Art, University of Pennsylvania, Philadelphia, *Grids* (January 27 – March 1)

Kunsthaus, Hamburg, *Gedok / American Women Artists Show* (April 14 – May 14)

University Art Museum, University of California, Berkeley, *Eight New York Painters* (May 10 – June 25)

The Aldrich Museum of Contemporary Art, Ridgefield, CT, *Paintings on Paper* (September 17 – December 17)

The Detroit Institute of Arts, Detroit, *12 Statements – Beyond the Sixties* (September 27 – November 5)

Fine Arts Center, University of Rhode Island, Kingston, *Three Artists: Mary Heilmann, Joan Snyder, Pat Steir* (February)

1972-73 The Kenan Center, Lockport, NY, *Ten Artists Who Happen To Be Women* (November 17, 1972 – January 14, 1973) (exhibition traveled to Michael C. Rockefeller Arts Center Gallery, Fredonia, NY (January 19 – February 18)

1973 Whitney Museum of American Art, New York, *1973 Whitney Biennial Exhibition: Contemporary American Art* (January 10 – March 18)

The New York Cultural Center, New York, *Women Choose Women* (January 12 – February 18)

Whitney Museum of American Art, New York, *American Drawings 1963-1973* (May 25 – July 22)

Stamford Museum and Nature Center, Stamford, CT, *Image of Movement* (June 22 – July 22)

The Art Gallery, Norfolk, CT, *Norfolk 73: An Exhibition of Paintings, Prints, Photographs, and Drawings by Resident Faculty of the Art Division of the Yale University Summer School of Music and Art* (June 24 – July 15)

Contemporary Arts Center, Cincinnati, *Options 73/30, Recent Works of Art* (September 25 – November 11)

1973-74 Saidye Bronfman Centre, Montreal, *28 Painters of the New York Avant-Garde / 28 Peintres de l'avant-garde New-Yorkaise* (November 27, 1973 – January 3, 1974)

1974 Pratt Institute Gallery, Pratt Institute, Brooklyn, *Recent Abstract Painting* (February 21 – March 15)

San Francisco Museum of Art, San Francisco, *The Levi Strauss Collection* (March 15 – April 14)

Museum of the Philadelphia Civic Center, Philadelphia, *Woman's Work – American Art 1974* (April 27 – May 26)

Michael Walls Gallery, New York, *Ten Painters in New York* (June 15 – July 6)

Institute of Contemporary Art, Boston, *Joan Snyder / Pat Steir* (October 1 – November 12)

1975 The Corcoran Gallery of Art, Washington, DC, *34th Biennial of Contemporary American Painting* (February 22 – April 6)

Frederick S. Wight Art Gallery, University of California, Los Angeles, *14 Abstract Painters* (March 25 – May 25)

Michael Walls Gallery, New York, *Thirty Artists in America*, Part I (June 7 – July 3)

1976 Fine Arts Gallery, State University of New York, Brockport, *Recent Abstract Painting* (February 8 – March 5)

Marion Koogler McNay Art Institute, San Antonio, *American Artists 76* (May 23 – July 31)

The Bronxton Gallery, Westwood, CA, *Joan Snyder / Laurence Fink* (June 1 – 26)

1977 Carl Solway Gallery, New York (May)

The Brooklyn Museum Art School, Brooklyn, *Contemporary Women – Consciousness and Content* (October 1 – 27)

Susan Caldwell, Inc., New York, *Drawing on a Grid: Eva Hesse, Agnes Martin, Katherine Porter, Joan Snyder* (October 5 – 29)

Douglass College, Rutgers, The State University of New Jersey, New Brunswick, *Twelve from Rutgers* (November – December)

The Women's Caucus for Art, Los Angeles, *Contemporary Issues: Works on Paper by Women*

1978 Freedman Gallery, Albright College, Reading, PA, *Perspective '78: Works by Women* (October 8 – November 15)

Harold Reed Gallery, New York, *A Benefit for the Yale School of Art: Works by Members of the Yale Faculty 1950-1978* (October 19 – November 19)

1979 Susan Caldwell, Inc., New York, *Generation: Twenty Abstract Painters Born in the United States Between 1929 and 1946* (February 2 – March 3)

Nielsen Gallery, Boston, *The Implicit Image: Abstract Painting in the Seventies* (April 29 – June 1)

Hamilton Gallery, New York, *Color and Structure* (May 5 – June 2)

Louis Abrons Arts For Living Center, Henry Street Settlement, New York, *Exchanges I* (May 11 – June 8)

1979-81 The New Museum of Contemporary Art, New York, *The 1970s: New American Painting* (June 15, 1979 – February 10, 1981) (exhibition sponsored by the United States Information Agency (USIA) and traveled to venues in Belgrade; Budapest; Bucharest; Zagreb; Ljubljana; Rome; Copenhagen; Warsaw)

1980 Hamilton Gallery, New York, *New Work*
Brockton Art Museum-Fuller Memorial, New York, *Aspects of the 70's / Painterly Abstraction*

1981 Seigel Contemporary Art, New York, *Painters' Painters*
The Museum of Modern Art, New York, *New Works on Paper I*
Whitney Museum of American Art, New York *1981 Whitney Biennial*
Miami University Art Museum, Oxford, OH, *A Seventies Selection*
Douglass College, Rutgers, The State University of New Jersey, New Brunswick, *The Women Artists Series: Tenth Anniversary Retrospective Show*

1982 WWAC Gallery, Westport, CT, *Art of the 80s*
Hamilton Gallery, New York, *The Abstract Image*
Alexander F. Milliken Gallery, Inc., New York, *Fast*
Rutgers State Museum, Trenton, NJ, *Rutgers Master of Fine Arts 20th Century Anniversary Exhibition*
Institute of Contemporary Art, Virginia Museum, Richmond, *American Abstraction Now*

1983 Gimple Fils Ltd., London, *Stroke, Line and Figure*

1984 Sidney Janis, New York, *American Women Artists: Part II The Recent Generation*
Museum of Fine Arts, Boston, *Brave New Work*
Organization of Independent Artists, New York, *Nature as Image*
Turman Gallery, Indiana State University, Terre Haute, *The New Culture: Women Artists in the Seventies*
Art City, New York, *Aliens*
School of Visual Art, New York, *Heroic Poetic*
Nielsen Gallery, Boston, *Location*
Douglass College, Rutgers, The State University of New Jersey, New Brunswick, *Representative Works 1971-1984, Women Artists Series and Focused Fragments*

1985 Art City, New York, *Male Sexuality: Expressions and Perceptions* (January 24 – February 17)
Princeton University, Princeton, *A Decade of Visual Arts at Princeton: Faculty 1975-1985*
Malinda Wyatt Gallery, New York, *The Bridge and Tunnel Crowd*

1985-86 Stamford Museum and Nature Center, CT, *American Art: American Women* (December 15, 1985 – February 23, 1986)

1986 Summit Art Center, Summit, NJ, *Symbolic Expressions: Five Women Artists* (March 23 – April 29)
L.A. Louver, Los Angeles, *American European Painting and Sculpture 1986* (Part I: July 19 – August 16; Part II: August 21 – September 13)
R.C. Erpf Gallery, New York, *A Look at Painting* (September 6 – October 4)
Ruth Siegel Gallery, New York, *Square and . . . .* (November 11 – December 24)
The Portia Harcus Gallery, Boston, *Sleeping Beauty*
Simard Halm & Shee Gallery, Los Angeles, *Painterly Abstractions: Eight New York Artists*
Plymouth State College, Plymouth, NH, *Protest*

1986-87 The Museum of Fine Arts, Boston, *Boston Collects: Contemporary Painting and Sculpture*
Hirschl & Adler Modern, New York, *The Intuitive Line*
The Aldrich Museum of Contemporary Art, Ridgefield, CT, *A Contemporary View of Nature*
Christine Burgin Gallery, New York, *Work from the Seventies*

1987 Corcoran Gallery of Art, Washington, DC, *Corcoran Biennial* (April 11 – June 21)
The Portia Harcus Gallery, Boston, *Thanks for the Memories*
Nielsen Gallery, Boston, *Seven Women Artists*
Hirschl & Adler Modern, New York, *Therese Oulton, Norbert Prangenberg, Joan Snyder*
Michael Walls Gallery, New York, *Beyond Reductive Tendencies*

Mount Holyoke College Art Museum, South Hadley, MA, *A Graphic Muse* (exhibition traveled to Yale University Art Gallery, New Haven; Santa Barbara Museum of Art, Santa Barbara; Virginia Museum of Fine Arts, Richmond; Nelson-Atkins Museum of Art, Kansas City)
Nielsen Gallery, Boston, *New Work: Gallery Artists*
Queensborough Community College of the City University of New York, Bayside, *The Politics of Gender*
The Parrish Art Museum, Southampton, NY, *Drawing on the East End 1940-1988*
Mary Ryan Gallery, New York, *Prints by Contemporary American Women Artists*
Nielsen Gallery, Boston, *Summertime* (June – July)

1987-89 Beijing Art Institute, Beijing, and Nielsen Gallery, Boston, *Beijing / New York Works on Paper*

1988 Nielsen Gallery, Boston, *Common Ground 1*

1989 Watkins Gallery, American University, Washington, DC, *Joan Snyder and Jane Wilson*
Hillwood Art Gallery, Long Island University, Brookville, *Lines of Vision: Drawings by Contemporary Women*
Ruth Siegel Gallery, New York, *Small and Stellar*
Nielsen Gallery, Boston, *Summertime* (June – July)
Nielsen Gallery, Boston, *Invitational, Small Paintings*
The Cincinnati Art Museum, Cincinnati, *Making Their Mark: Women Artists Move into the Mainstream 1970-85* (exhibition traveled to the New Orleans Museum of Art, New Orleans; Denver Art Museum, Denver; The Pennsylvania Academy of the Fine Arts, Philadelphia)

1990 Rose Art Museum, Brandeis University, Waltham, MA, *The Image of Abstract Painting in the '80s*
Museum of Fine Arts, Boston, *The Unique Print / 70s into 90s*
Victoria Munroe Gallery, New York, *Selected Works on Paper*
Nielsen Gallery, Boston, *Summertime*

1991 Baumgartner Galleries, Inc., Washington, DC, *The Figure in the Landscape*
Proctor Art Center, Bard College, Annandale-on-Hudson, NY, *Drawings By . . .*
Vrej Baghoomian Gallery, New York, *Figuring Abstraction*
The Mills Gallery, Boston Center for the Arts, Boston, *Nuclear Solstice*
American Academy and Institute of Arts and Letters, New York, *43rd Annual Academy-Institute Purchase Exhibition*

1992 Gibbes Museum of Art and the School of the Arts, College of Charleston, Charleston, SC, *Painting Self Evident: Evolutions in Abstraction*
Nielsen Gallery, Boston, *In the Spirit of Landscape*
Edward Thorpe Gallery, New York, *Paint*
Pamela Auchincloss Gallery, New York, *Contemporary Surfaces*
Artists Space, New York, *Putt-Modernism*
Michael Walls Gallery, New York, *Intimate Universe*
Mabel Smith Douglass Library, Douglass College, Rutgers, The State University of New Jersey, New Brunswick, *The Twentieth Year Representative Invitational Show*

1993 Victoria Munroe Fine Art, New York, *Works on Paper: Lyric with an Edge*
Rubelle and Norman Schafler Gallery, Pratt Manhattan Gallery, New York, *Abstraction Per Se*

1994 Jay Gorney Modern Art, New York, *Joan Snyder / Jessica Stockholder* (January 8 – February 12)
Center for the Fine Arts, Miami, *Abstraction: A Tradition of Collecting in Miami*
Robert McClain & Co., Houston, *Art and Social Conscience*
On Crosby Street, New York, *Isn't It Romantic?*
The Parrish Art Museum, Southampton, NY, *Mirrors*
Academy of Arts and Letters, New York, *46th Annual American Academy Purchase Exhibition*
Art Initiatives at Tribeca, 148 Gallery, New York, *Poetic Heroic: Twelve American Artists*
Bixler Gallery and Cynthia McCallister Gallery, New York, *To Enchant (blue)*

Midtown Payson, New York, *Trees*

1995 O'Hara Gallery, New York, *A Romantic Impulse: Seventeen American Artists*

The Painting Center, New York, *Painting: The Intimate View*

Marsh Art Gallery, University of Richmond, Richmond, VA, *Repicturing Abstraction* [jointly organized by the Richmond Curatorial Project]

O'Hara Gallery, New York, *The Small Painting*

Elena Zang Gallery, Shady, NY

1996 Galerie Françoise, Baltimore, *Joan Snyder / Josh Dorman, A Mentor Show*

Elena Zang Gallery, Shady, NY, *Miniatures by Major Artists*

University of Rhode Island, Kingston, *The Uneasy Surface: Points of Turbulence*

Nielsen Gallery, Boston, *5 Women / 5 Rooms* [M. Gallace, A. Harris, A. Lemieux, J. Snyder, N. Spero]

Edward Thorp Gallery, New York, *Epitaphs*

Art Initiatives, New York, *(Ap)praising Abstraction*

Mason Gross School of the Arts Galleries, Rutgers, The State University of New Jersey, New Brunswick, *Fifteen Degrees from Rutgers, Charting New Directions in Contemporary Art*

Andre Zarre Gallery, New York, *Moderate Fable: Homage to Marguerite Young*

Nielsen Gallery, Boston, *Still Life / Still Alive*

Milwaukee Art Museum, Milwaukee, *Ink on Paper: The Quad / Collection, 1971-1996*

Hirschl & Adler Modern, New York, *Summer Exhibition*

CRG Gallery, New York, *La Toilette de Venus*

Rutgers, The State University of New Jersey, New Brunswick, *Mary H. Dana, Women Artists Series, 25 Years 1971-1996* (October)

1997 Sleeth Gallery, West Virginia Wesleyan College, Buckhannon, *Uncommon Threads: Weaving Narrative and Collaboration* (January) [Prints from Rutgers Center for Innovative Print and Paper]

Santa Barbara Contemporary Arts Forum, Santa Barbara, CA, *20/20: CAF Looks Forward and Back* (February 15 – April 13)

The Newhouse Center for Contemporary Art, Snug Harbor, Staten Island, NY, *After the Fall: Aspects of Abstract Painting Since 1970* (March 30 – June 29)

Nielsen Gallery, Boston, *In the Spirit of Landscape II* (June 7 – August 2)

The Work Space, New York, *Lilith* (August 13 – October 11)

Rider University Gallery, Lawrenceville, NJ, *Abstract Tendencies* (September 11 – October 12)

Jan Abrams Fine Art, New York, *Women Artists of the 70s* (September 24 – November 1)

Gallery 128, New York, *Material Girls: Gender, Process and Abstract Art Since 1970* (October 1 – November 1)

Elena Zang Gallery, Shady, NY, *Joan Snyder, Judy Pfaff, Mary Frank*

Elena Zang Gallery, Shady, NY, *Flowers*

Robert Steele Gallery, New York, *Intimate Universe (Revisited)*

The Art Museum at Florida International University Miami, *American Art Today: The Garden*

1998 Art Resources Transfer @ Fred Dorfman, New York, *Tip of the Iceberg* (January 8 – February 15)

Jay Gorney Modern Art, New York, *Group Exhibition* (January 17 – February 7)

Locks Gallery, Philadelphia, *Flowers in Mind* (February 6 – March 7)

Butler Institute of American Art, Youngstown, OH, *Master of the Masters* (April 5 – May 17) [exhibit of MFA faculty of the School of Visual Arts, 1983-1998]

Brenda Taylor, New York, *Objects of Desire* (June 6 – July 11)

The Parrish Art Museum, Southampton, NY, *Dreams for the Next Century: A View of the Collection* (July 25 – September 6)

Smack Mellon Studios, Brooklyn, *Just Ripe* (November 7 – December 20)

Riva Yares Gallery, Scottsdale, AZ, *Theatre of Art III* (November 14 – December 31)
Hirschl & Adler Modern, New York, *Summer Hours*
Elena Zang Gallery, Shady, NY, *Miniatures*

1998-99 Museum of Fine Arts, Boston, *Reflections of Monet* (September 19, 1998 – January 19, 1999)
Art Complex Museum, Duxbury, MA, *Immortalized* (November 15, 1998 – January 24, 1999)

1998-01 Ashville Museum of Art, Ashville, NC, *Beyond the Mountains: The Contemporary American Landscape* (March 19 – May 31) (exhibition traveled to Newcomb Art Gallery, Tulane University, New Orleans (December 1, 1999 – February 13, 2000); Muskegon Museum of Art, Muskegon, MI (February 26 – April 9); Polk Museum of Art, Lakeland, FL (May 27 – August 6); Boise Art Museum, Boise, ID (August 12 – October 22); Ft. Wayne Museum of Art, Ft. Wayne, IN (November 18, 2000 – January 14, 2001); Lyman Allyn Museum at Connecticut College, New London)

1999 Nielsen Gallery, Boston, *Then and Now: 35th Anniversary Exhibition* (January 9 – February 20)
DC Moore Gallery, New York, *The Likeness of Being: Contemporary Self Portraits by 60 Women Artists* (January 12 – February 5)
Fine Arts Center Galleries, University of Rhode Island, Kingston, *Unlocking the Grid* (January – February)
Times Square Gallery, Hunter College MFA Building, New York, *Immediacies of the Hand: Recent Abstract Painting in New York* (February 25 – April 17)
Jim Kempner Fine Art, New York, *Women in Print* (March 6 – April 11)
Smack Mellon Studios, Brooklyn, *Red Square* (May 1 – June 25)
Sheehan Gallery, Walla Walla, WA, *Contemporary Collaborations, The Artist and the Master Printer* (August 27 – September 24)

1999-00 Aronson Gallery, Parsons School of Design, New York, *Drawing in the Present Tense* (October 13 – December 3, 1999) (exhibition traveled to Eastern Connecticut State University, Willimantic (January 7 – February 27, 2000)
Whitney Museum of American Art at Champion, Stamford, CT, *Contemporary Narratives in American Prints* (November 18, 1999 – February 2, 2000)

2000 Contemporary Gallery, Marywood University, Scranton, PA, *Nature: Contemporary Art and the Natural World* (March 25 - April 16)
Pamela Hamilton, Los Angeles, *Mysticism and Desire*
Nielsen Gallery, Boston, *In the Spirit of Landscape V*
The Jewish Museum, New York, *The Perpetual Well: Contemporary Art from the Collection of The Jewish Museum* (exhibition traveled to Samuel P. Harn Museum of Art, University of Florida, Gainesville; Sheldon Memorial Art Gallery and Sculpture Garden, University of Nebraska, Lincoln; The Parrish Art Museum, Southampton, NY; Huntington Museum of Art, Inc., Huntington, WV)
Nielsen Gallery, Boston, *Rooms*
Nielsen Gallery, Boston, *New Work*
DC Moore Gallery, New York, *The Likeness of Being: Contemporary Self Portraits by Sixty Women*
Ceres Gallery, New York, *Lives and Works: The Exhibition*

AWARDS

1974 National Endowment for the Arts Fellowship
1983 John Simon Guggenheim Memorial Fellowship

SELECTED PUBLIC COLLECTIONS

Allen Art Museum, Oberlin College, Oberlin, OH
Allentown Art Museum, Allentown, PA
American Can Company, Greenwich, CT
BankAmerica Corporation, San Francisco
Ball State University Museum of Art, Muncie, IN
Chase Manhattan Bank, New York
The Corcoran Gallery of Art, Washington, DC
Dallas Museum of Art, Dallas
First Church of Christ Scientist, Boston
Fogg Art Museum, Harvard University Art Museums, Cambridge, MA
Frederick R. Weisman Museum of Art, Pepperdine University, Malibu, CA
Grand Rapids Art Museum, Grand Rapids, MI
High Museum of Art, Atlanta
J.B. Speed Art Museum, Louisville, KY
The Jewish Museum, New York
The Metropolitan Museum of Art, New York
The Museum of Fine Arts, Boston
The Museum of Modern Art, New York
The National Museum of Women in the Arts, Washington, DC
Neuberger Museum of Art, Purchase College, State University of New York, Purchase
The Phillips Collection, Washington, DC
Prudential Life Insurance Corporation, Newark
Reeds Hill Foundation, Carlisle, MA
Rose Art Museum, Brandeis University, Waltham, MA
Smith College Museum of Art, Northampton, MA
United Bank of California, Los Angeles
Virginia Museum of Fine Arts, Richmond
The Walker Hill Art Center, Seoul, Korea
Whitney Museum of American Art, New York
Wichita Art Museum, Wichita, KS
Worcester Art Museum, Worcester, MA

BIBLIOGRAPHY

1963 Brown, Doris. "Young Artist Finds Inspiring Riverfront Studio." *New Brunswick*, March 31, p. 40.

1971 Frankenstein, Alfred. "Powerful, Roughhewn Paintings." *San Francisco Chronicle*, August 28, p. 36.

Linville, Kasha. "Group Show: Paley and Lowe Gallery." *Artforum*, vol. 9, no. 5, January, p. 81, illus. [*Romantic Renewal Mechanisms*, 1970, reproduced, p. 80].

Robbin, Tony. "A Protean Sensibility." *Arts Magazine*, vol. 45, no. 7, May, pp. 28-30, illus. [*Symphony*, 1970, reproduced, p. 29].

Stiles, Knute. "Joan Snyder, Michael Walls Gallery." *Artforum*, vol. 10, no. 3, November, pp. 87-88.

Tucker, Marcia. "The Anatomy of a Stroke: Recent Paintings by Joan Snyder." *Artforum*, May, pp. 42-45, illus. [*Big Green*, 1970, reproduced, p. 42; *First Anniversary*, 1970, reproduced, p. 43; *Whole Segments*, 1970, and *Symphony*, 1970, reproduced, p. 44].

1972 Baker, Kenneth. *The Christian Science Monitor*, April 20, p. 8, illus. [*Symphony*, 1970, and *No Skeleton for Evsa*, 1971, reproduced, p. 8].

Borden, Lizzie. "Joan Snyder, Paley and Lowe Gallery in New York." *Artforum*, vol. 10, no. 5, January, pp. 88-89, illus. [*No Skeleton for Evsa*, 1971, reproduced, p. 88].

Davis, Douglas. "Portrait of Young Artists." *Newsweek*, February 7, p. 79.

Elderfield, John. "Grids." *Artforum*, vol. 10, no. 5, May 9, pp. 52-59.

____. "The Whitney Annual." *Art in America*, vol. 60, no. 3, May-June, pp. 27, 29, illus. [*Smashed Strokes Hope*, 1972, reproduced, p. 27].

Hickey, Dave. "Frankenthaler at Emmerich; Joan Snyder at Paley & Lowe." *Art in America*, vol. 60, no. 1, January-February, pp. 33, 35.

Hughes, Robert. "Myths of Sensibility." *Time*, March, pp. 72-77, illus. [*Smashed Strokes Hope*, 1972, reproduced, p. 73].

Ratcliff, Carter. "New York Letter." *Art International*, vol. 16, no. 1, January 20, p. 68, illus. [*No Skeleton for Evsa*, 1971, reproduced, p. 45].

1973 Alloway, Lawrence. "Joan Snyder's New Paintings." *The Nation*, vol. 4, no. 216, June 4, pp. 732-733.

Anderson, Laurie. "Joan Snyder's Recent Paintings at Paley & Lowe." *ARTnews*, vol. 72, no. 5, May, p. 91.

Davis, Douglas. "A Spring Sampler of Shows." *Newsweek*, April 30, pp. 88-89, illus. [*The Stripper*, 1973, reproduced, p. 72].

____. "Art Without Limits." *Newsweek*, December 24, pp. 68-74.

Kingsley, April. "Women Choose Women." *Artforum*, vol. 11, no. 7, March, pp. 69-73.

Schjeldahl, Peter. "Joan Snyder - The Energy and Surprise Have Gone." *The New York Times*, May 13, p. D23, illus. [*Moonshine for D, L and M*, 1973, reproduced, p. D23].

1974 Bell, Jane. "Ten Painters in New York." *Arts Magazine*, vol. 49, no. 2, October, p. 62, illus. [*The Storm*, 1974, reproduced, p. 62].

Snyder, Joan. Untitled statement. *Studio International Journal of Modern Art*, July-August, illus. [*Moonshine for D, L and M*, 1973, and *The Stripper*, 1973, reproduced, p. 32].

1975 Snyder, Joan. "Painters Reply." *Artforum*, vol. 14, no. 1, September, pp. 26-36, illus. [*Creek Square*, 1974, reproduced, p. 33].

1976 Herrera, Hayden. "Joan Snyder at Carl Solway." *Art in America*, vol. 64, no. 3, May-June, pp. 103-104, illus. [*Vanishing Theater*, 1974-75, reproduced, p. 103].

Ratcliff, Carter. "The Paint Thickens." *Artforum*, vol. 14, no. 10, June, pp. 43-47.

Webster, Sally. "Joan Snyder, Fury and Fugue, Politics of the Inside." *Feminist Art Journal*, vol. 5, no. 2, Summer, p. 5.

1977 Bell, Jane. "Drawing, Now, Then, and Again." *New York Arts Journal*, no. 7, November-December, pp. 13-14.

Iskin, Ruth. "Interview with Joan Snyder." *Chrysalis*, no. 1, pp. 101-115.

1978 Kramer, Hilton. "Other Exhibitions This Week." *The New York Times*, March 3, p. C18.

Rubinfien, Leo. "Joan Snyder, Hamilton Gallery." *Artforum*, vol. 16, no. 10, Summer, pp. 74-75, illus. [*Boat Painting*, 1977-78, reproduced, p. 75].

Shirey, David L. "Spirited Feminist Wields Bold Brush." *The New York Times*, February 12, section 22, p. 2.

Welish, Marjorie. "Joan Snyder at Hamilton." *Art in America*, vol. 66, no. 4, July-August, p. 114, illus. [*Resurrection*, 1977, reproduced, p. 114].

1979 Bell, Jane. "Generation (Susan Caldwell)." *ARTnews*, vol. 78, no. 4, April, pp. 154, 156.

Russell, John. "Generation: An Invitational Exhibition (Susan Caldwell Gallery)." *The New York Times*, February 9, p. C24.

1980 Merritt, Robert. "Art: Joan Snyder." *Richmond Times-Dispatch*, May 8, p. E13.

1982 Cohen, Ronny. "Joan Snyder." *Artforum*, vol. 21, no. 1, September, p. 81.

Henry, Gerrit. Joan Snyder at Hamilton." *Art in America*, vol. 70, no. 6, Summer, p. 142.

____. "Expressionism Today: An Artists' Symposium". *Art in America*, December.

Herrera, Hayden. "Expressionism Today: An Artists' Symposium: Joan Snyder." *Art in America*, vol. 70, no. 1, December, p. 58.

Merritt, Robert. "Art Review: American Abstraction Now." *Richmond Times-Dispatch*, September 2, p. E9.

1983 Temin, Christine. "Joan Snyder's Totems." *Boston Globe*, May 12.

1985 Gardner, Paul. "When Is a Painting Finished?" *ARTnews*, November, pp. 89-99.

Gill, Susan. "Joan Snyder, Hirschl & Adler Modern." *ARTnews*, vol. 84, no. 10, December.

Schwabsky, Barry. "Joan Snyder." *Arts Magazine*, vol. 60, no. 4, December, p. 108.

1986 Henry, Gerrit. "Joan Snyder: True Grit." *Art in America*, vol. 74, no. 2, February, pp. 96-101, illus. [*Bedeckt mich mit Blumen*, 1985, reproduced, p. 96; *Can We Turn Our Rage to Poetry*, 1985, reproduced, pp. 98-99; *The Field / May*, 1985, reproduced, pp. 100-101].

Keyes, Norman. [Review]. *Boston Globe*, October 24.

Perl, Jed. "Houses, Fields, Gardens, Hills." *New Criterion*, vol. 4, no. 6, February, pp. 43-49.

[Review]. *The New York Times*, February 7.

1987 Brenson, Michael. "True Believers Who Keep the Flame of Painting." *The New York Times*, June 7.

Gill, Susan. "Painting From the Heart." *ARTnews*, vol. 86, no. 4, April, pp. 128-135.

Klein, Ellen Lee. "Therese Oulton / Norbert Prangenberg / Joan Snyder." *Arts Magazine*, vol. 62, no. 2, October, p. 111.

Tarlow, Lois. "Joan Snyder: Interview." *Art New England*, February.

1988 Harrison, Helen A. "Poles of Expression: Formal and Emotional." *The New York Times*, December 4.

Larson, Kay. "The Art of Diplomacy." *New York Magazine*, April 11, pp. 115-116.

Loughery, John. "Joan Snyder." *Arts Magazine*, vol. 62, no. 10, Summer, p. 105.

McCracken, David. "Snyder Paints to Try to Heal the Children." *Chicago Tribune*, December 9.

Perl, Jed. "The Joans of Art." *Vogue*, March, p.110.

____. "Gallery-Going." *New Criterion*, vol. 6, no. 10, June, pp. 70-71.

Sherman, Mary. "Joan Snyder Evokes Big Issues." *Chicago Sun-Times*, December 9.

Smith, Roberta. "Artworks That Strike Up Conversations with Viewers." *The New York Times*, April 1.

1989 Crowder, Joan. "A Very Personal Retrospective of Painting." *Santa Barbara News Press*, January 20.

Gamble, Allison. "Reviews." *New Art Examiner*, vol.16, no.7, March, p.44.
Muchnic, Suzanne. "Two Views of the 'Renewal' of the Abstract." *Los Angeles Times*, January 24.

1990 Cotter, Holland. "Joan Snyder at Hirschl & Adler Modern." *Art in America*, vol. 78, no. 10, October, p. 215.
Grove, Nancy. Review in "Juggling Acts." *Art and Antiques*, vol. 7, no. 4, April, pp. 131-132.
Jones, Bill. "Joan Snyder." *Arts Magazine*, Summer, p. 76.
Parks, Addison. "Art Weighted with Emotion." *Christian Science Monitor*, November 15.
Perl, Jed. "Mixed Media." *New Criterion*, vol. 8, no. 8, April, pp. 52-54.
Ratcliff, Carter. "Notes on Line." *Art in America*, no. 78, no. 6, June, pp. 152-157.
Smith, Roberta. "Joan Snyder." *The New York Times*, February 23.
Stapen, Nancy. "Abstract is Back." *The Boston Herald*, April 5.
Temin, Christine. "Abstraction Puts On a New Face in the 80s." *Boston Globe*, April 23.

1991 Dilorio, Marisa. "An Interview with Joan Snyder." *Q: A Journal of Art* [Department of Art, College of Architecture, Art and Planning, Cornell University], May, pp. 32-35.
McQuaid, Cate. "Apocalyptic Art." *South End News*, July 25-31.
Pacheco, Patrick. "The New Faith in Painting." *Art and Antiques*, April; pp. 56-67.
Snyder, Joan. "Passages." *Modern Painters*, vol. 4, no. 2, Autumn, pp. 48-49.
Stapen, Nancy. "Passion Fuels 'Nuclear Solstice'." *Boston Globe*, July 5.
____. "Images from the Unconscious." *Boston Globe*, October 25.
Tallman, Susan. "Many Monotypes." *Arts Magazine*, vol. 65, no. 5, January, pp. 17-18.

1992 Cotter, Holland. "In Orbit Amid Black Silk." *The New York Times*, October 30.
____. "Contemporary Surfaces." *The New York Times*, August 7.
Neely, Anne. "Nielsen Gallery / Boston, Joan Snyder; New Paintings." *Art New England*, vol. 14, no. 2, February/March.
Snyder, Joan. "It Wasn't Neo to Us." *The Journal of the Rutgers University Librairies*, June, vol. 54, no. 1, pp. 34-35.
____. "Being a Mother." *Meaning*, no. 12, November, pp. 36-37.

1993 Cohen, Terri. "Narratives: Joan Snyder and Rena Bransten." *Artweek*, vol. 24, no. 11, June, p. 18.
Hackett, Regina. "Seattle Exhibits Art Fair's Best." *Seattle Post-Intelligencer*, February 6.
Perl, Jed. "Getting Emotional." *New Criterion*, February p.52.
Stapen, Nancy. "Elusive Moments Captured in Paint." *Boston Globe*, April 22.

1994 "Art: The 10 Best Shows of 1994." *New York Magazine*, December 19-24.
Braff, Phyllis. "The Restlessness & Imagination of·2 Important Pioneers." *The New York Times*, July 31, p.16.
Cotter, Holland. "Taking it Personally: Putting Emotions on Paper." *The New York Times*, April 8, p. C26.
Cross, Jennifer. "An Artist's Tribute to the Act of Painting." *The Southampton Press*, August 11, p. B1.
Graf, Roberta. "The Human Experience in Art." *South Shore Record*, August 4.
Harris, Susan. "Joan Snyder, Jessica Stockholder." *Art Press*, March, p. 85.
Herrera, Hayden. "Who Are the Most Underrated and Overrated Artists? " *ARTnews*, February 1, p. 110.
____. "Joan Snyder Traffics in Art and True Grit. " *The New York Times*, July 24, p.32, illus. [*The Cherry Tree*, 1994, reproduced, p. 32].
Hess, Elizabeth. "Fem Fatale. " *Village Voice*, January 25, p.82.
Jones, Bill. "Painting the Haunted Pool. " *Art in America*, October, pp. 120ñ123, 157, illus. [Reproductions of *Red Field*, 1993, p. 120; *Satin Core Metaphor (Dedicated to Maggie)*, 1992, & *A Place . . . For You*, 1993, both p. 121; *The Changing Nature of Grief*,

1992, pp. 122-123; *Summer Painting 1991*, 1991, p. 123].

Kimmelman, Michael. "Joan Snyder and Jessica Stockholder. " *The New York Times*, February 4.

Kuspit, Donald. "Joan Snyder at Hirschl & Adler Modern." *Artforum*, Summer, pp. 92-93.

Perl, Jed. "Snyder's Earth, Freud's Skin. " *New Criterion*, February, pp. 51-54 .

Schnore, Peter. "Joan Snyder: Works With Paper." *Art Matters*, December 1993 - January 1994, p. 4.

Slivka, C.S. Rose. "From the Studio." *The East Hampton Star*, August 18, p. 119.

Smith, Roberta. "To Enchant (blue)." *The New York Times*, July 22, p. C24.

____. "Building on the Bare, Bare Bones. " *The New York Times*, August 12, p. C22.

Snyder, Joan. Essay for "Light, Canvas, Action! (When Artists Go to the Movies)." *ARTnews*, December, p. 129.

Stapen, Nancy. "The Emotion Packed Paintings of Joan Snyder." *Boston Globe*, April 22.

Stevens, Mark. "10 Best shows of 1994. " *New York Magazine*, December, p. 132.

Wiess, Marion Wolberg. "Parrish Art Museum" *Dan's Papers*, August 12, p. 91.

1995 "Awards: Best Regional Show of 1994." *Art in America*, May, p. 134.

Guidon, Andrew. "Joan Snyder: Artist at Work." *Park Slope Journal*, February, p. 4.

Kasrel, Deni. [Review]. *Philadelphia Business Journal*, June 9-15.

Samuels, Renee. "Joan of Art." *The Woodstock Times*, September 28, cover page, p. 12.

Sozanski, Edward J. "Joan Snyder at Locks Gallery." *The Philadelphia Enquirer*, May 26.

1996 Bowyer, Bell, J. "Joan Snyder." *Review*, vol. 1, no. 1, April 1, p. 13.

Cotter, Holland. "Joan Snyder. " *The New York Times*, May 3, p.C28.

Freda, Elise Andkjar. "Passion in Paint: A Profile of Willow's Joan Snyder." *Art in the Valley*, Autumn, pp. 4-5.

Horowitz, Stash. "A Room of Her Own." *The Back Bay Courant*, February 6, sec. 11.

Kolva, Jeanne. "Borough Native's Artwork on Display at Zimmerli." *Highland Park Herald*, June 28, p. A3.

____. "A Treasure Trove of World Art." *Highland Park Herald*, July 10-12, p. B5.

Maniaci, Cara. "A Quintet of Artistic Expression." *The Tufts Daily*, January 31.

McQuaid, Cate. "A Wealth of Art from Women." *Boston Globe*, February 1.

Perl, Jed. "Abstract Matters." *The New Republic*, June 10, pp. 25-30.

Schwabsky, Barry. "Distinguished Alumni Help Rutgers Inaugurate Its New Arts Center. " *The New York Times* (New Jersey edition), March 3, p. 7.

Sherman, Mary. "Rooms with Five Views." *The Boston Herald*, January 26.

Watkins, Eileen. "Rutgers Artists Throw Housewarming Party." *Star Ledger* [Newark, NJ], March, pp. 39, 50.

1997 Berger, Laurie. "In Their Sights." *ARTnews*, vol. 96, no. 3, March, p. 98.

Cotter, Holland. "An Era Still Driven to Abstraction." *The New York Times*, April 11, p. C22.

Fressola, Michael. "Driven by Abstraction." *Staten Island Advance*, June 15, p.3.

____. "Obviously, Painting is Alive and Well 'After the Fall'." *Staten Island Advance*, April 11.

McQuaid, Cate. "Snyder's Paintings from the Heart." *Boston Globe*, December 12, p. C12.

Mendelsohn, John. "The Abstract Lilith." *The Jewish Week*, August 29, p. 14.

Wilkinson, Jeanne C. "After the Fall: Aspects of Abstract Painting Since 1970." *Review Art*, May 15, p. 11.

1998 "Arts Watch." *MS.*, March-April.

Cohen, Joyce. "Joan Snyder." *Art New England*, February-March.

Gambino, Erica-Lynn. "Ambitious Exhibition." *The Southampton Press*, August 13.

Johnson, Ken. "Joan Snyder." *The New York Times*, May 8, p. E32.

Klein, Mason. "Joan Snyder: Hirschl & Adler Modern." *Artforum*, October, p. 126.
Klein, Michael. "Joan Snyder: Works on Paper." *Artnet*, May 1.
Murdock, Robert M. [Review] of two exhibitions: BMA and Hirschl & Adler Modern]. *Review* , May 1, pp. 7-8.
Nagy, Peter. "Beach Arty." *Time Out,* August 6-13, p. 51.
Perl, Jed. "Seeing and Time." *The New Republic*, August 3, pp. 31-37.
Sweeney, Matthew. "Emotion Etched in Her Art." *The Brooklyn Papers*, March 6, p. 7.
Unger, Miles. "Joan Snyder." *ARTnews*, March, p. 177.
1999 Cotter, Holland. "Immediacies of the Hand." *The New York Times*, April 9, p. C2.
Duffy, Peter. "Spice Warehouse Gets Artsy." *Brooklyn Bridge*, May, p. 29.
Esplund, Lance. "Blood, Sweat and Tears." *Modern Painters*, Autumn, illus. [*Oratorio*, 1997, reproduced in color].
Everett, Deborah. "Review: Hunter College's Times Square Gallery." *NY Arts*, vol. 4, no. 3, p. 58, illus.
McQuaid, Cate. "Nielsen Gala Sees Artists as Evolving Souls." *Boston Globe*, February 4.
Perl, Jed. "Jed Perl on Art: Dream Team." *The New Republic*, June 14, pp. 32-34, 36, illus. [*Oratorio*, 1997, reproduced in color].
Shulman, Ken. "Then & Now." *ARTnews*, May, p. 172.
Tarlow, Lois. "Turning Points." *Art New England*, vol. 21, no. 1, December-January, pp. 24-26.
Temin, Christine. "Artists Share Feelings About Their Dearly Departed." *Boston Globe*, January 8.
Van Siclen, Bill. "URI's 'Unlocking the Grid' Releases Creativity." *The Providence Journal*, February 19, p. E8.
Wallace, Gregory. "Unlocking the Grid: Concerning the Grid in Recent Painting." *Art New England*, April/May, p. 53.
2000 Youens, Rachel. "The Likeness of Being." *NY Arts*, vol. 5, no. 1, p. 49.

BOOKS AND CATALOGUES

1972 Elderfield, John. *Grids* (exhibition catalogue). Philadelphia: Institute of Contemporary Art.
Kolbert, Frank L. *12 Statements: Beyond the 60s* (exhibition catalogue). Detroit: The Detroit Institute of Arts. [*Womanchild*, 1972, reproduced, unpaginated].
Lippard, Lucy. "Top to Bottom, Left to Right." *1972 Annual Exhibition: Contemporary American Painting* (exhibition catalogue). New York: Whitney Museum of American Art.
____. "Why A Women's Art Show." *Ten Artists Who Happen To Be Women* (exhibition catalogue). Lockport, NY: The Kenan Center. [*Brown / Gold*, 1970, reproduced, unpaginated].
Paintings On Paper (exhibition catalogue). Ridgefield, CT: The Aldrich Museum of Contemporary Art.
Picard, Lil. *Gedok American Woman Artist Show* (exhibition catalogue). Hamburg: Kunsthaus, p. 37. [*Me and Marcia*, 1971, reproduced, p. 37].
1973 Baur, John. I. H. *1973 Whitney Biennial Exhibition* (exhibition catalogue). New York: Whitney Museum of American Art. [*Womanchild*, 1972, reproduced, p. 76].
Boulton, Jack. *Options 73 / 30: Recent Works of Art* (exhibition catalogue). Cincinnati: Contemporary Arts Center. [*Moonshine for D, L. and M,* 1973, reproduced, unpaginated].
Dyens, Georges, and Marcia Tucker. *28 Painters of the New York Avant-Garde / 28 Peintres de l'avant-garde New-Yorkaise* (exhibition catalogue). Montreal: The Saidye Bronfman Centre. [*Moonshine for D, L. and M,* 1973, reproduced, unpaginated].
Image of Movement (exhibition catalogue). Stamford: CT: Stamford Museum and Nature Center [*Resolve in Four by Eight,*1972, reproduced, unpaginated].
Lippard, Lucy. "A Note on the Politics and Aesthetics of a Women's Show." *Women Choose Women* (exhibition catalogue). New York: The New York Cultural Center.
Norfolk 73: An Exhibition of Paintings, Prints,

Photographs and Drawings by the Resident Faculty of the Art Division of the Yale University Summer School of Music and Art (exhibition catalogue). Norfolk, CT: The Art Gallery.

Solomon, Elke M. *American Drawings 1963-1973* (exhibition catalogue). New York: Whitney Museum of American Art. [*Untitled*, 1972, reproduced, p. 50].

1974 Baker, Kenneth. "Joan Snyder." *Joan Snyder and Pat Steir* (exhibition catalogue). Boston: Institute of Contemporary Art. [*Summer Painting*, 1971, *Layer Take*, 1972, and *Houses*, 1972, reproduced, unpaginated].

Hayes, Gerald. *Recent Abstract Painting* (exhibition catalogue). Brooklyn: Pratt Institute. [*Squares*, 1972, reproduced, unpaginated].

Hopkins, Henry T. *The Levi Strauss Collection* (exhibition catalogue). San Francisco: San Francisco Museum of Art. [*Untitled*, 1972, reproduced, unpaginated].

1975 Nordland, Gerald. *Fourteen Abstract Painters* (exhibition catalogue). Los Angeles: Frederick S. Wright Art Gallery, University of California, Los Angeles. [*The Storm*, 1974, reproduced, p. 31].

Slade, Roy. *34th Biennial of Contemporary American Painting* (exhibition catalogue). Washington, DC: The Corcoran Gallery of Art. [*Creek Square*, 1974, reproduced, p. 95].

1976 Hayes, Gerald. *Recent Abstract Painting* (exhibition catalogue). Brockport, NY: Fine Arts Gallery, State University of New York. [*Then Is Now*, 1974, reproduced, unpaginated].

Herrera, Hayden. *Joan Snyder* (exhibition catalogue). Century City: Los Angeles Institute of Contemporary Art. [*The Storm*, 1974, *Vanishing Theatre*, 1974-75, *Symphony III*, 1975, *Me and Marcia*, 1971, *Houses*, 1972, *Small Symphony for Women*, 1974, and *Symphony II*,1974, all reproduced].

Lippard, Lucy. *Women Artists Series, Year Five* (exhibition catalogue). New Brunswick, NJ: Mabel Smith Douglass Library, Douglass College.

Simkins, Alice C. *American Artists '76: A Celebration* (exhibition catalogue). [*Untitled*, 1974, reproduced, unpaginated].

1977 Bell, Jane. "Joan Snyder." *Contemporary Artists* (exhibition catalogue). Ed. Colin Naylor, and Genesis P. Orridge. London: St. James Press & New York: St. Martin's Press, pp. 893-894. [*Mom's Just Out There Tryin' To Break That Grid*, 1975, reproduced, p. 894].

Wechsler, Jeffrey. *Twelve from Rutgers* (exhibition catalogue). New Brunswick, NJ: Rutgers University Art Gallery.

1978 Forge, Andrew. *A Benefit Exhibition for the Yale School of Art: Works by Members of the Yale Faculty 1950-1978* (exhibition catalogue). New York: Harold Reed Gallery. [*Untitled*, 1972, reproduced, unpaginated].

Herrera, Hayden. *Joan Snyder: Seven Years of Work* (exhibition catalogue). Purchase, NY: Neuberger Museum of Art, Purchase College, State University of New York, Purchase.

Perspective '78: Works by Women (exhibition catalogue). Reading, PA: Albright College. [*Rooms*, 1977, reproduced, p. 53].

1979 Lippard, Lucy R. *Exchanges of What? Esthetic Energy? Style? Prestige? Power? Best Wishes?* (exhibition catalogue). New York: Louis Abrons Arts for Living Center, Henry Street Settlement.

Thomas, Kathleen, and Allan Schwartzman. *The 1970s: New American Painting* (exhibition catalogue). New York: The New Museum, for the International Communication Agency. [*Farm Landscape*, 1977, reproduced].

Walls, Michael. *Joan Snyder* (exhibition catalogue). San Francisco: San Francisco Art Institute.

1981 Elderfield, John. *New Work on Paper 1* (exhibition catalogue). New York: The Museum of Modern Art.

Hanhardt, John, et al. *1981 Whitney Biennial Exhibition* (exhibition catalogue). New York: Whitney Museum of American Art.

1984 Janis, Sidney. *American Women Artists; Part 1: 20th Century Artists* (exhibition catalogue). New York: Sidney Janis Gallery.

1985 Baker, John. *Joan Snyder* (exhibition catalogue). New York: Hirschl & Adler Modern.
Rosenbaum, Allen, and James Seawright. *A Decade of Visual Arts at Princeton: Faculty 1975-1985* (exhibition catalogue). Princeton: The Art Museum, Princeton University.

1986 Halm, Will, and Charles Kessler. *Painterly Abstraction* (exhibition catalogue). Los Angeles: Simard Halm & Shee Gallery.
Yau, John. *A Contemporary View of Nature* (exhibition catalogue). Ridgefield, CT: The Aldrich Museum of Contemporary Art.

1987 Rifkin, Ned, and Jane Livingston. *Corcoran Biennial Exhibition of Contemporary American Painting* (exhibition catalogue). Washington, DC: Corcoran Gallery of Art.
Therese Oulton, Norbert Prangenberg, Joan Snyder (exhibition catalogue). New York: Hirschl & Adler Modern.

1988 Baker, John. *Joan Snyder* (exhibition catalogue). New York: Hirschl & Adler Modern.
Hererra, Hayden. *Joan Snyder Collects Joan Snyder* (exhibition catalogue). Santa Barbara: Santa Barbara Contemporary Arts Forum.
Kertess, Klaus. *Drawing on the East End, 1940-1988* (exhibition catalogue). Southampton: The Parrish Art Museum.
Malen, Lenore. *The Politics of Gender* (exhibition catalogue). Queens, NY: The QCC Art Gallery, Queensborough Community College.

1990 Ackley, Clifford S. *The Unique Print / 70s into 90s* (exhibition catalogue). Boston: Museum of Fine Arts.
Snyder-Fink, Molly. *Joan Snyder* (exhibition catalogue). New York: Hirschl & Adler Modern.

1991 Ashton, Dore. *Joan Snyder* (exhibition catalogue). Boston: Nielsen Gallery.
Hannan, Greg. *The Figure in the Landscape* (exhibition catalogue). Washington, DC: Baumgartner Galleries, Inc.

1992 Ackley, Clifford S. *Abstraction per se* (exhibition catalogue). New York: Pratt Manhattan Gallery & Brooklyn: Pratt Institute.
Phillips, Michael. *Painting Self Evident / Evolutions in Abstraction* (exhibition catalogue). Charleston, SC: Gibbs Museum of Art, College of Charleston.
Snyder, Joan, Beryl K. Smith, David Carr, Joan Marter, and Ferris Olin. *The Twentieth Year Representative Invitational Show* (exhibition catalogue). New Brunswick, NJ: Rutgers, The State University of New Jersey, New Brunswick.

1993 McNear, Sarah Anne. *Joan Snyder Works with Paper* (exhibition catalogue). Allentown, PA: Allentown Art Museum.

1994 Belz, Carl. *Joan Snyder* (exhibition catalogue). Waltham, MA: Brandeis University.
Kramer, Trudy. *Mirrors* (exhibition catalogue). Southampton, NY: The Parrish Art Museum.
Rubinstein, Raphael. *Isn't It Romantic?* (exhibition catalogue). New York: One Crosby Street.
Schjeldahl, Peter, and Jackson Rushing. *Abstraction: A Tradition of Collecting in Miami* (exhibition catalogue). Miami: Center for the Fine Arts.

1995 Diehl, Carol. *Joan Snyder* (exhibition catalogue). Philadelphia: Locks Gallery.
Repicturing Abstraction (exhibition catalogue). Richmond: Virginia Museum of Fine Arts.

1996 *Mary H. Dana, Women Artists Series, 25 Years 1971-1996* (exhibition catalogue). New Brunswick: Rutgers, The State University of New Jersey, New Brunswick.
Smith, Beryl, Joan Arbeiter, and Sally Shearer Swenson. *Lives and Works, Talks with Women Artists*, vol. 2. Lanham, MA: The Scarecrow Press, Inc.

1997 Naves, Mario. *American Art Today: The Garden* (exhibition catalogue). Miami: The Art Museum at Florida International University.
Rosenthal, Deborah, and Lance Esplund. *Abstract Tendencies* (exhibiton catalogue). Lawrenceville, NJ: Rider University Gallery.
Uncommon Threads, Weaving Narrative and Collaboration (exhibition catalogue). Buckhannon, WV:

Sleeth College, West Virginia Westeyan College.

1998 *Joan Snyder Painting and Sketches* (exhibition catalogue). New York: Hirschl & Adler Modern.

Shirey, David L. *Master of the Masters* (exhibition catalogue). Youngstown, OH: Butler Institute of American Art.

Wei, Lily. *After the Fall* (exhibition catalogue). Staten Island: Snug Harbor Cultural Center.

1999 Balken, Debra Bricker. *Drawing in the Present Tense* (exhibition catalogue). New York: Parsons School of Design, and Willimantic, CT: Eastern Connecticut State University.

Ratcliff, Carter, and Kim Sobel. *Immediacies of the Hand: Recent Abstract Painting in New York* (exhibition catalogue). New York: Hunter College of The City of New York.

2000 Snyder-Fink, Molly. *Joan Snyder: In Times of Great Disorder* (exhibition catalogue). Boston: Nielsen Gallery.

Heller, Nancy G., et al. *Women Artists. Works from the National Museum of Women in the Arts.* New York: Rizzoli International Publications, Inc., and Washington, DC: National Museum of Women in the Arts, pp. 200-201. [*Can We Turn Our Rage to Poetry*, 1985, reproduced in color, pp. 200-201.]

Klein, Michael. *Beyond the Mountains: The Contemporary American Landscapes* (exhibition catalogue). New Orleans: Newcomb Art Gallery, Tulane University.

Stein, Judith E. *The Likeness of Being: Contemporary Self Portraits by Sixty Women* (exhibition catalogue). New York: DC Moore Gallery.

2001 Snyder, Joan. *Joan Snyder: Primary Fields* (exhibition catalogue). New York: Robert Miller Gallery.

This catalogue accompanies the exhibition

JOAN SNYDER: PRIMARY FIELDS

April 25 - May 26, 2001

ROBERT MILLER GALLERY

524 West 26 Street, New York, NY 10001

Catalogue coordinated by Christopher R. Miller

Biography and Bibliography coordinated by Randy White

Photography by Steven Sloman, New York and Adam Reich, New York

Edited by Amy Young and Randy White

Produced in a limited edition of 2,000 copies

AGW Lithographers, New York

Published by Robert Miller Gallery

ISBN # 0-944680-63-1